Amazing KITCHEN CHEMISTRY

Projects You Can Build Yourself

Cynthia Light Brown

Illustrated by Blair Shedd

Nomad Press
A division of Nomad Communications
10 9 8 7 6 5 4 3 2
ISBN: 978-1-9346700-6-4

Illustrations by Blair Shedd; image on page 19 courtesy of M.A. Quilliam, National Research Council Canada

Questions regarding the ordering of this book should be addressed to
Independent Publishers Group
814 N. Franklin St.
Chicago, IL 60610
www.ipgbook.com

Nomad Press
2456 Christian St.
White River Junction, VT 05001

green press
press
INITIATIVE

To Bob and Audrey, amazing parents, who gave me my first chemistry set and my first love of science.

Acknowledgments

I am greatly indebted to many people for ideas, reviews, interviews, insight, corrections, encouragement, endorsements, you name it. Any errors are all mine, but there are far fewer thanks to the following people: Dr. Stephen Bates, Research Scientist, Fisheries and Oceans Canada; Dr. Michael Quilliam, Research Scientist, Institute for Marine Biosciences, Canada; Dr. Irwin Rose, Professor-in-Residence, University of California Irvine and 2004 Nobel Prize winner in Chemistry; Dr. John Mainstone, Professor of Physics, University of Queensland; Dr. Anne Hall, Research Scientist at Lovelace Respiratory Research Institute and former high school chemistry teacher; Dr. Roald Hoffmann, Professor of Chemistry, Cornell University and 1981 Nobel Prize winner in Chemistry; Dr. Peter Agre, Vice Chancellor for Science and Technology, Duke University and Nobel Prize winner in Chemistry; Dr. Robert Deegan, Research Scientist, University of Bristol, U.K.; Dr. Andrea Hoyt Haight, Research Scientist, Adherent Technologies; science teachers Mike Young, Kevin McCann, Jonathan Ptachcinski, and Robin Patrick; and colleague Greg McCall and Carlie McGinty. To my critique group—Andrea, Carol, Coleen, Dave, Julie, Judy, Kitty, Marcy, Pat, and Susan—thanks for all of the questions and tweaks. Thanks to my younger friends, who concocted all manner of things—Alex, Ava, Grace, Katie, Megan, Michael, Morrin, Nick, Skip, and Susan. To the whole staff of Nomad Press and my agent, Caryn Wiseman, thanks for your hard work and patience. And finally, to my husband Phil, thanks for putting up with a disastrous kitchen and always supporting me.

CONTENTS

Other titles from Nomad Press

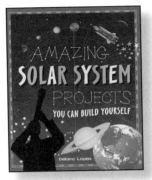

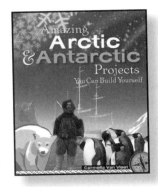

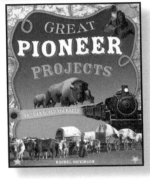

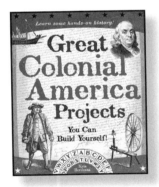

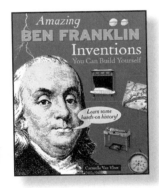

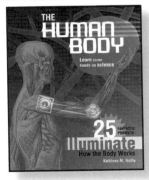

Chemistry is at the heart of how everything works; it's the science of change. What makes something soft or hard, or a solid, liquid, or gas? **Chemistry** tells you. It also looks at what makes something explode or freeze, sizzle and pop, or not change at all, because it's about how those **substances** interact and change.

Introduction
How to Use This Book

You can experiment with materials in your own kitchen to discover and learn the answers to these questions. You'll make goop, cause **chemical reactions,** and create yummy treats, and each project will illustrate an important chemical concept. You can go through the chapters in order or just dive into a particularly interesting project and see where it leads. All of the materials you will use can be found in your own kitchen or at a local grocery store, drugstore, or hardware store. You can do most of the projects with little help from an adult.

A Roman philosopher named Seneca once wrote, "Luck is what happens when preparation meets opportunity." Although he lived about 2,000 years ago, what he said then is still true.

This could be *your* lucky day. You can make new discoveries, create a tasty treat, or devise a new "magic" trick. But you have to be prepared. You have to have the right materials, the right setup, and, most of all, the right attitude. With these three things you'll learn as much as you can, as safely as you can, and with as much fun as possible.

The Mind of a Scientist

Scientists have a special way of looking at looking at the world, and you can too. Here's what you do.

Notice things. Pay attention! Look around you! If Benjamin Franklin hadn't noticed how the water changed behind ships as they sailed, he wouldn't have experimented with oil and water. If you notice what's going on around you, you'll see all kinds of things to investigate and explore.

Investigate! If you see something you don't understand or that doesn't make sense, find out more about it. That may involve some research in a library, but it might also involve trying an experiment, which is another important—and even more fun—way to investigate. Ask questions, like "Why?" and "What would happen if . . .?"

After you try an experiment or a project in this book, you can also change the experiment a bit to see what happens. (If you want to use new materials, though, check with an adult first to make sure the experiment will be safe.)

WORDS TO KNOW

chemistry: the study of the properties of substances and how they react with one another.

substance: physical material from which something is made.

chemical reaction: the rearragement of atoms in a substance to make a new chemical substance.

ENGLISH? METRIC?

You may notice that throughout the book, when a quantity of something is given, there is another number and unit in parentheses. For example: one inch (2.5 centimeters). The first number and unit is using the English system of measurement, and the number and unit in parentheses is using the metric system, which is the measuring system used by scientists throughout the world, including scientists in the United States. Most of the world uses the metric system for everything, but in the United States, most things are measured using the English system. More and more, people use the metric system in the United States—every hear of a 2-liter soda bottle? Or megabytes of memory for a computer? That's metric! But, especially in the kitchen, the English system is still used a lot, such as tablespoons and cups. So we give both measurements! What are the advantages of using the metric system? It's based on a decimal system, that is, powers of ten. So it's much easier to multiply and divide the numbers. Because it's used throughout the world, it's also easier to be able to communicate with others. That's especially important for scientists, because the scientific community is really a worldwide community—when a scientist does an experiment, the results are shared with scientists everywhere, who can then build on that work with more experiments.

TOOLS AND MATERIALS

Some materials are specific to one or just a few experiments, but some things are used over and over. You may decide to keep a special corner or box as your science lab, so your basic tools and materials are right at hand. Here are some standard tools:

- notebook and pencil
- candy thermometer
- weather thermometer
- plastic and glass bottles and jars
- paper towels and soap
- measuring cups/spoons
- safety goggles
- paper and scissors

Here's the important thing about making changes in a project: **only make one change at a time**. Otherwise, you won't know which of your changes made a difference in the results.

Believe what you see, not what you think you should see. If Erasto Mpemba hadn't believed his own eyes, he never would have figured out that boiling water can freeze faster than warm water. When you try an experiment or make a change to one you've already done, try to predict what might happen next. Even if your results aren't what you expected, you can learn something. If something doesn't work the way you expected, maybe you made a mistake. For example, you might have put in too much of one ingredient. But maybe your results show you something new. Scientists make new discoveries all the time based on "mistakes."

Share and compare. Scientists often work together to solve problems. If Harry Kroto, Rick Smalley, and Bob Curl hadn't worked together as a team, they probably wouldn't have discovered the buckyball or won the Nobel Prize. Keep track of your results and share them with others. Maybe together you can figure out why your project or experiment turned out like it did.

DID YOU KNOW?

In 1999, the unmanned Mars Climate Orbiter was lost because two different measuring systems were used in its engineering. The engineering team that programmed the software sending information to the Orbiter used the English system, but the team that programmed the Orbiter to receive the information used the metric system. Because of the mismatch in units, the Orbiter entered Mars' orbit too low, and vanished. The Orbiter was designed to help understand the history of water and the potential for life on Mars—and it cost $125 million!

3

Play It Safe

These experiments are designed to be safe, but you still have to be careful. Every laboratory, or "lab," has rules and so does yours. Here they are.

- Make sure an adult knows what you're doing, where you're working, and what you're using.

- If an experiment involves very hot stuff, like boiling water or making candy, **get an adult to help you!** You can still be in charge and run the experiment, but let your grown-up "lab assistant" handle the hot stuff. Not only will this keep you safe, but it has the added advantage that you get to boss around the adult. Make sure there are plenty of potholders nearby.

- Read the instructions for a project or experiment all the way through and make sure you have all of the materials **before** you begin. There may be some items that you need to get at the grocery store, drugstore, or hardware store.

- If there's a small child or pet in your house, be extra careful not to leave small or sharp objects or any liquids (including glue) within their reach. For this reason, it's best to do your experiments on a kitchen counter or table.

- Wash your hands before and after each project.

- If a project needs to sit overnight or without your supervision (like crystal making), put a label on it, place it where it won't be disturbed, and make sure it's not within reach of small children or animals.

- When you're finished, make sure everything is completely cleaned up and put away, the stove is turned off, and there are no chemicals left around.

- Don't pour any goopy substances down the sink. Throw them in the trash.

- If you try any variations on these projects or make up your own new experiments, get an adult to look over what you're doing. A good rule of thumb: it's safe to mix food items together, but it is not safe to mix cleaning materials together.

- If you're not sure if something is safe, stop what you're doing and ask an adult.

So get your mind in gear and your supplies in order. You'll have so much fun ma' these projects, you may not even notice how much you're learning. And after y tried all of the experiments and projects in this book, make up your own. You'r charge, so get ready to **Build It Yourself!**

A star. The air. A roly-poly bug. Clouds. Hot lava. Icebergs. You. All of these things have different shapes, colors, temperatures, textures, and densities. In other ways, though, they're all the same. They are all made up of relatively few kinds of particles. It's the arrangement of those particles that makes all the difference in the world. It even makes all the difference in the universe.

Atoms & Molecules
Don't Sweat the Small Stuff

Atoms are the basic building blocks of everything. They are very tiny—so tiny that you can't even see them with most microscopes. Every atom is composed of **protons**, **neutrons**, and **electrons**. The protons have a positive **electrical charge**, the electrons have a negative charge, and the neutrons don't have a charge—they are neutral. The protons and neutrons clump together in the **nucleus**, or center, of the atom, and the electrons spin around the nucleus.

WORDS TO KNOW

atom: the smallest particle of matter that cannot be broken down by chemical means. An atom is made up of a nucleus of protons and neutrons, surrounded by a cloud of electrons.

proton: a type of elementary particle that has a positive electrical charge and is found in the nucleus of all atoms.

neutron: a particle of an atom that has no electrical charge and is found in the nucleus of all atoms.

electron: a stable, negatively charged particle found in all atoms.

electrical charge: a fundamental property of matter. Protons and the nuclei of atoms have a positive charge, electrons have a negative charge, and neutrons have no charge. Normally, each atom has as many protons as electrons and thus has no net electrical charge. In other words, the atom is neutral.

nucleus: the central part of an atom, made up of protons and neutrons.

nuclear reaction: a process in which two nuclei or nuclear particles collide to produce products different from the initial particles.

THIS IS THE BEST REPRESENTATION OF AN ATOM...

...OR IS IT?

Years ago, people thought that electrons travel around the nucleus in definite circular patterns, or orbits. You may have seen pictures like this. Now we know that electrons don't follow a perfect circle around the nucleus but are more likely to go around in certain places. A famous physicist named Erwin Schrödinger said the electron is like a "vibrating string." If you took a picture of all of the places that electrons go, it would look like a cloud, like the drawing below. The electrons do orbit in shells, which are regions of space around the nucleus. If you think of the nucleus as a beehive, then the electrons would be the bees swarming around it.

The nucleus is held together very tightly—so tightly, in fact, that it takes a **nuclear reaction** to split one. But the electrons aren't held as tightly, so it's easier to add an electron to an atom or take away an electron from an atom. And those electrons don't always like to stay in one place. Electrons have a negative charge and are attracted to protons, which have a positive charge. So electrons often move around, sticking to protons in other atoms. It is this movement of electrons that allows atoms to bond together to make all of the different substances in and around you. And that's what chemistry is all about.

Elements

We call a substance that is made up of just one type of atom an **element**. Pure gold, for example, only has one type of atom. There are 92 different kinds of atoms, or elements, that occur naturally. All **matter**, from the smallest speck to the largest star, is made of these elements.

What makes the difference between different kinds of elements is the number of protons in the nucleus of its atom. A hydrogen atom, for example, always has one proton. An oxygen atom always has eight protons. And a gold atom always has 79 protons.

THE ANCIENT GREEKS

Around 440 BCE—that's over 2,400 years ago—Greek philosophers tried to understand the nature of the universe. They didn't do much in the way of experiments, but they did ask a lot of questions and debate answers. Two of these philosophers, a man named Democritus and his teacher, Leucippus, asked what would happen if you cut a block of silver in half, then cut the half in half, and just kept doing this. They thought that eventually you would get to the smallest particle of silver, which couldn't be cut anymore, and they called those particles atoms. Atom is Greek for something that cannot be divided. They also said that those atoms are always moving, and because they need space to move in, there must also be empty space, or a **void**. So far, so good. But according to Democritus and Leucippus, there was an infinite variety of atoms, so a tree was made of completely different stuff than air.

Of course, not everyone agreed with them. Aristotle was a brilliant Greek philosopher who contributed much to scientific understanding, but he got some things wrong too when it came to atoms. He said that if you kept dividing silver, you would never finish, so there couldn't be any such thing as an atom. He and other Greek philosophers developed the idea that all matter was made of four elements—earth, air, water, and fire—and these elements could be changed from one into another. Even though Aristotle had the number of elements wrong, he had the right idea about a relatively small number of elements combining in different ways to make up all matter.

WORDS TO KNOW

element: a substance whose atoms are all the same. Examples of elements include gold, oxygen, and carbon.

matter: the material substance of the universe that has mass, occupies space, and can change (convert) into energy.

void: a large hole or empty space.

molecule: the simplest structural unit of an element or compound, a group of atoms bonded together. Molecules can break apart and form new ones, which is a chemical reaction.

bond: an attractive force that holds together the atoms, ions, or groups of atoms in a molecule or crystal.

ion: an atom that has an unequal number of protons and electrons. Ions have either a positive or negative charge.

neon: a gas that gives an orange glow when electricity is passed through it, used in fluorescent lighting.

Molecules

Is there a water atom? No. Hardly anything is a pure element. Water, like most things, is made up of **molecules**. Molecules are simply two or more atoms bonded together. The atoms can be the same kind but more often are different types of atoms. The **bond** that holds them together isn't a fixed thing, like a stick or string, even though we draw it that way sometimes. A bond is a force, so the atoms can still wiggle, or vibrate, when they're bonded. There are different kinds of bonds, but all bonds have to do with atoms sharing or trading their electrons. Remember,

DID YOU KNOW?

The number of molecules you breathe in, in only one breath of air, is more than the number of grains of sand on the entire earth.

electrons like to travel, and because they are always moving around, we have not just 92 different kinds of natural substances but millions.

Ions

There are as many electrons as protons in each atom, so the electrons' negative charge and the protons' positive charge balance each other out. As a result, atoms have a neutral charge. **Neon** has 10 protons and 10 electrons. Some elements tend to gain or lose one or more electrons, but it's still the same element.

HOW SMALL IS A MOLECULE?

Molecules and atoms are so very tiny that it's hard to even imagine them. A single grain of sugar contains about 1,000,000,000,000,000,000—or a quintillion—molecules. How big is a **quintillion**? If each molecule was the size of a penny, then a grain of sugar would be as wide and long as a football field, with pennies stacked almost 100,000 miles (160,000 kilometers) high. That would be almost halfway to the moon. Think about the size of the cavity that you'd get from that much sugar!

SWEET!

Hydrogen, for example, tends to lose its electron. It's still hydrogen, but without its electron it has a positive charge. When an atom has lost or gained an electron and has a positive or negative charge, we call it an **ion**.

Chemical Formulas

If you had to write a math equation, you probably wouldn't write, "Twenty-eight plus fourteen equals forty-two." It would take too long to write and it would be hard to read quickly. You would write, "$28 + 14 = 42$." Chemistry is the same way. Chemists have to write chemical equations all the time, and it would take too long to write and read if they had to spell everything out. So chemists use symbols, just like we do in math.

Each element has a symbol. There's a particular way of writing what's in a molecule, called a **chemical formula**. The chemical formula lists all the elements that form each molecule and uses a small number to the bottom right of an element's symbol to stand for the number of atoms of that element. For example, the chemical formula for water is H_2O. That tells us that a water molecule is made up of two hydrogen ("H" and "2") atoms and one oxygen ("O") atom.

DID YOU KNOW?

Diamonds are the hardest natural substance known.

Carbon

Diamonds, when cut, are sparkly and beautiful. They are also the hardest substance known. Graphite, which is used in pencils, is dull and gray and so soft you can write with it. About as different as you can get, right?

GIANT MOLECULES

Just how complicated can carbon-based molecules be? Take a look at **hemoglobin**, which is what makes blood red. Hemoglobin is the part of blood that carries oxygen from our lungs to the rest of our body; without it, we couldn't live. The chemical formula for hemoglobin is $C_{2954}H_{516}N_{780}O_{806}S_{12}Fe_4$. That's 2,954 atoms of carbon ("C"), 516 atoms of hydrogen ("H"), 780 atoms of nitrogen ("N"), 806 atoms of oxygen ("O"), 12 atoms of sulfur ("S"), and 4 atoms of iron ("Fe" for ferrum, which is Latin for iron). All of that is in each hemoglobin molecule, and all of those atoms are arranged in a very specific way. That's one complex molecule!

Wrong. Diamonds and graphite are very much alike. They are both made of exactly the same thing: **carbon**. And nothing else. In fact, when graphite is deep in the ground, under pressure for a long time, it can turn into diamond.

The reason diamonds and graphite have such different qualities is not because of what they're made of but because of how all of that carbon is put together. If you could shrink to the size of an atom and walk around inside a diamond and a piece of graphite, they would look quite different to you. Each carbon atom in diamonds is joined to four others to make a **tetrahedron**, and all of the bonds are strong. You can see the triangle shape of the tetrahedron in the model to the left, and triangles are very strong shapes.

DID YOU KNOW?
A nanotube i 50,000 times thinner than a human hair.

MODEL OF GRAPHITE.

MODEL OF DIAMOND.

In graphite, the carbon atoms bond in rings of six, or **hexagons**, which form sheets of carbon. The sheets look like a honeycomb and are very strong—as strong as diamonds—but the bonds between the sheets are very weak, and break easily. When the weak bonds break, the sheets slide against each other and separate. When you write with your pencil, some of the graphite is breaking off to make a mark. You are leaving a trail of carbon behind on the paper.

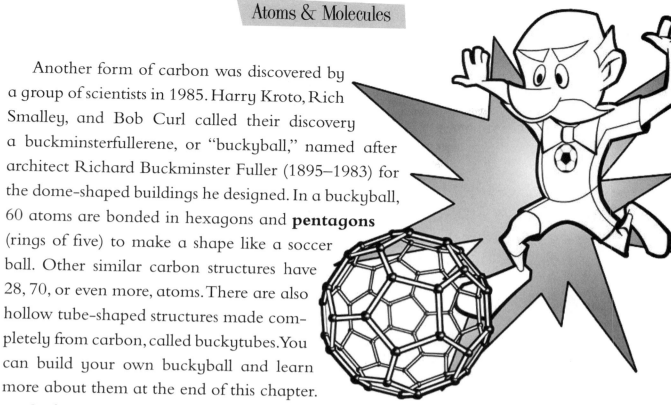

Another form of carbon was discovered by a group of scientists in 1985. Harry Kroto, Rich Smalley, and Bob Curl called their discovery a buckminsterfullerene, or "buckyball," named after architect Richard Buckminster Fuller (1895–1983) for the dome-shaped buildings he designed. In a buckyball, 60 atoms are bonded in hexagons and **pentagons** (rings of five) to make a shape like a soccer ball. Other similar carbon structures have 28, 70, or even more, atoms. There are also hollow tube-shaped structures made completely from carbon, called buckytubes. You can build your own buckyball and learn more about them at the end of this chapter.

Carbon is the most important atom in living creatures. Without it, life—at least, life as we know it—could not exist. This is because carbon can form huge, complicated molecules or almost endless chains. Living things need these complicated molecules because they have to accomplish a huge variety of tasks. No matter how it's put together, carbon is a strange and wonderful substance.

WORDS TO KNOW

quintillion: The cardinal number with 18 zeroes after it.

chemical formula: a representation of a substance or of a chemical reaction using symbols for its elements.

hemoglobin: a substance in red blood cells that combines with and carries oxygen around the body, and gives blood its red color.

carbon: an element found in all living things.

tetrahedron: a shape with four triangular faces.

hexagon: a plane figure with six straight sides and angles.

pentagon: a plane figure with five straight sides and angles.

Make Your Own
BUCKYBALL

1 Poke one toothpick into two gumdrops of the same color. The gumdrops represent the carbon atoms, and the toothpick represents the bonds between them.

2 Poke another toothpick into one of the gumdrops a little bit more than 90 degrees from the first toothpick. Add a gumdrop of the same color to the end of the second toothpick.

3 Repeat step 2 until there are five toothpicks. For the fifth toothpick, don't add a gumdrop, but poke the toothpick into the first gumdrop. You should have a pentagon shape (a five-sided shape) of toothpicks and gumdrops.

4 Make 11 more pentagons of toothpicks and gumdrops. One pentagon should be the same color as the first one, and the other 10 should use a different color of gumdrop. All of the gumdrops represent the same kind of atom—carbon—but it's easier to put them together if you use two different colors.

5 Place the pentagon of the first color flat on a table. Place five pentagons of the second color around it at each of the five points. Using a toothpick, join each gumdrop in the center pentagon to one of the other pentagons.

+Supp[L]ies

- packages of toothpicks
- at least 60 small gumdrops, in at least two colors

12

6 Join each of the outer pentagons to the one next to it with a toothpick. Each of your links should make a hexagon, or six-sided shape. As you put in toothpicks, the whole structure will bend to make a bowl shape.

7 Repeat steps 1–6 with more gumdrops and toothpicks. To finish the buckyball, join the two bowls together into a ball. The edges of the bowls are uneven, with two gumdrops sticking out next to two that don't stick out. Offset these sticking out parts between the two sides. Link the two sides so that all of these new links form hexagons.

What's Happening?

You have made a model of a buckyball. A buckyball is made of only carbon atoms. Does the shape remind you of anything? If you have a soccer ball handy, look at it closely. A soccer ball has the same shape as a buckyball: 12 pentagons and 20 hexagons. This structure makes buckyballs extremely strong—stronger even than diamonds!

Since the discovery of buckyballs on September 14, 1985, researchers have been working to discover ways to use them to do useful things. One of the unusual things about buckyballs is that they are hollow but enclosed, like a cage, and they can trap other atoms inside. Researchers are exploring whether buckyballs could be used to carry or hold other atoms in a way that's useful.

Other materials that are related to buckyballs are buckytubes, which are hollow tubes made of carbon, and buckypaper, which is made from buckytubes. Because all of these "bucky" materials are so different from other molecules, there may be ways they can be used that would be completely new, unlike any technology we have now. Or they may be able to do things better and for less money than other materials, like conducting electricity and making better armor for soldiers.

Make Your Own
MODEL OF A WATER MOLECULE

1 Poke a toothpick into the orange. Hold the toothpick between your thumb and forefinger and poke the other side into a cherry.

2 Poke another toothpick into the orange a little bit more than 90 degrees away from the first. If the orange was a clock, and the first cherry was at 12:00, poke the second toothpick at 4:00. Poke the second cherry in the same way as the first.

What's Happening?

You have just made a model of a water molecule. The model of water is like a real molecule in some ways: there is one atom of oxygen and two atoms of hydrogen, and they are positioned at an angle to each other like your model. The oxygen atom takes up much more space than the hydrogen atoms, just like in your model. But in other ways, the model is different. Atoms aren't held together by sticks. They are held together by a force, more like magnets that get close to each other. Real atoms don't have a round, solid shape like the orange and cherries. Usually, a model of something is much smaller than the real thing, like a toy car is much smaller than a real car. But your model is much, MUCH larger than a molecule.

- one orange
- two cherries or cherry tomatoes
- 2 toothpicks

A pure substance is one in which all the molecules are the same. Pure gold doesn't have anything else mixed in but gold. Sugar is made of only one kind of molecule. Most things aren't pure, though. Even the water you drink isn't pure. It has many other kinds of molecules in it besides H_2O—like fluoride, which is added to help make your teeth stronger. Pure is good, but things get a lot more interesting when pure substances are combined to make mixtures.

Mix It Up With
Mixtures

A **mixture** is just that—a substance that has different materials mixed together. In some mixtures, you can see the different parts, like pebbles of different sizes and colors mixed together. Look closely at a piece of wood; do you see light and dark parts? Can you think of other mixtures you can see? For most mixtures, though, you can't see the different parts because they are mixed as molecules, which are too small to see. The molecules are side by side—they aren't bonded together.

MIXTURES ARE YUMMY!

Some mixtures are simple. Salt water is just the water molecule with sodium chloride (salt) mixed in. A penny is zinc and copper mixed together. Chocolate looks simple. A plain chocolate bar is all one color, all the same texture, and it seems to melt all at once. You might think it's all made up of one type of molecule, maybe even called the chocolate molecule. Or perhaps it's a simple mixture of two types of molecules.

Chocolate is anything but simple, though. A study of one type of chocolate found 57 different **compounds** in it. That means your yummy chocolate bar has 57 different types of molecules all mixed up together. It's that complex mixture that gives chocolate its delicious, rich taste.

I LOVE THIS KIND OF SCIENCE!

Imagine a huge room full of people, some wearing white shirts, which we'll call white atoms, and the others wearing black shirts, which we'll call black atoms. Each white atom has locked its arms, or bonded, with two black atoms, and all of these groups are moving around the room. Sometimes the groups bump into each other, but they don't unlock their arms or join arms with anyone else. Each group is like a molecule and all the molecules are the same, so the room is a pure substance.

Now imagine that there are two kinds of groups. Some groups are the same as before, one white atom and two black atoms. Other groups are just two white atoms with their arms locked together. Each group is like a molecule, but even though the same atoms are used, the molecules aren't the same. The room is a mixture.

In case you're thinking that mixtures are boring, think again. When things are mixed together, their **properties** change, sometimes unexpectedly. Steel can be made harder or more flexible, depending on what other materials are mixed in. Adding salt to water makes it taste different and also makes it freeze at a lower temperature. Can you think of other mixtures that change the properties of a material? Mixtures can be solid, liquid, or gas. Without mixtures, we wouldn't have ice cream, or grass, or stars, or life, or even chocolate!

Science Detectives Are on the Case

Chemists are detectives. They figure out what's in stuff, how that stuff changes, and why. When chemists have a material and they don't know what it is, the first thing they do is separate the mixture into pure substances. Then they figure out what the pure substances are. But how do you know if it's a mixture?

It's easy to tell that something is a mixture when you can see the different parts, like a mixture of pebbles that are different sizes. Often, though, something looks like it's a pure substance when it's really a mixture.

Try this: Pour a little whole milk into a cup and let it sit on the counter for three or four days. After several days, look carefully at the milk. Can you see small white blobs? Milk might look like a pure substance, but to a chemist, it's not pure. It's a mixture. The white blobs you see are the fat particles that are separating from the rest of the milk mixture. Don't forget to throw out the milk afterwards!

So how can we separate out the different parts? Some of the ways chemists, including chemists like you, can separate out mixtures are by color, shape, size, density, or the temperature at which they melt or evaporate. Any difference between the different parts can be used. Try some of these ways in the projects at the end of this chapter.

WORDS TO KNOW

pure substance: a substance where all of the molecules are the same, such as pure gold or a quartz crystal.

mixture: a substance that has two or more different kinds of materials mixed together but not bonded together. A mixture can be separated by mechanical means, like filtering or evaporation. Air, muddy water, or brass—a mixture of zinc and copper—are mixtures.

compound: a substance made up of two or more elements. The elements are held together by bonds just as molecules are held together by bonds. Compounds are not easily separated. Water is a compound.

properties: unique characteristics of a substance.

chromatography: a method of separating the components of a mixture by differences in their attraction to a liquid or gas.

neurotoxic: poisonous to nerves or nerve tissues, like the brain.

ALL THAT FAT IS IN ME?

FROM NOW ON, I MAKE SKIM ONLY!

CRAZY BIRDS, DEADLY MUSSELS,

In the middle of the night on August 18, 1961, people living in the coastal town of Capitola, California, woke to hear thousands of birds slamming into their homes. They rushed outside with flashlights, but the birds flew towards the lights, pecking at the people and sending them back inside, horrified. By dawn, the streets were covered with dead and stunned birds, and no one knew why. Alfred Hitchcock, a famous movie director, heard about what happened. Two years later, he made a thriller film called *The Birds*, which featured an invasion of attacking birds.

"It could be the most terrifying science experiment I've ever seen!"

NOT THE HAIR! PLEASE, NOT THE HAIR!

The Birds!

Twenty-six years later, another mysterious incident happened, this one on the Atlantic coast of Canada. Over 100 people got very sick after eating mussels, a type of shellfish. They were disoriented, confused, and some had seizures and memory loss. Three people died. No one knew exactly what was causing the problem but it was clear that scientists needed to find out why— quickly—before other people got sick. Whatever was in the mussels could show up again in seafood if they couldn't find out what it was or where it came from.

A team of more than 40 scientists assembled at the National Research Council of Canada to solve what came to be called the amnesic shellfish poisoning mystery. Scientists had already tested for bacteria, heavy metals, and pesticides that they knew could cause sickness, but none of these were the cause. The mussel samples were a mixture of thousands of different chemical compounds, and scientists didn't even know what many of them were. How can you separate out an unknown when you don't know what you're looking for or what its properties are?

Do you ever play 20 questions? So do scientists, except that scientists can ask as many questions as they need to. When you're playing 20 questions, you're trying to figure out what someone else is thinking of—the unknown. You start by asking about big categories, such as whether the unknown is a plant or an animal. Then, when the questioner answers, "Yes" or "No," you keep narrowing things down until you know what the unknown is.

That's what the scientists did to find out what was poisoning the people. They knew the poison was affecting the nervous system. They couldn't test it on people, but they discovered that small amounts of the poison injected into mice would cause them to scratch themselves. So if the mice scratched themselves

∗ND 20 QUESTIONS

after being injected, that would be like getting a "yes" to one of the 20 questions. They then separated the mixture based on certain properties and injected each part into the mice to see which part made the mice scratch.

For example, some compounds will dissolve in water and others in fat (called a lipid). One of their 20 questions was, "Does the poisoning agent dissolve in water or fat?" To get an answer, they shook one mussel sample with a mixture of water and another mussel sample with a mixture of fat and injected the water and fat parts into different mice. The part of the mussel that dissolved in the water still caused the mice to scratch themselves, but the part that dissolved in fat didn't. So they knew they were looking for a chemical that dissolves in water. They divided the mussel over and over using many different methods, including **chromatography**, which is similar to the project at the end of this chapter. Finally, after four days of continuous work, the scientists had separated out of the mixture a pure substance that was the toxic compound. They compared all of its properties to compounds they already knew about and found a match: a **neurotoxic** compound called "domoic acid."

Where had the domoic acid come from? The biggest clue was that it was only in the digestive system of the mussels, which were stuffed with phytoplankton. Phytoplankton, sometimes called algae, are microscopic one-celled plants that float in the ocean and provide food for many sea animals (as well as some of the oxygen we breathe). Most algae is perfectly safe, but as it turns out, a particular type of phytoplankton produces domoic acid, which can build up in sea creatures that eat this type of algae. The mussels had very high levels of domoic acid. Twenty-six years before, the birds in Capitola, California, had eaten anchovies, which had high concentrations of domoic acid from eating toxic algae. So the birds, like the people in Canada, had likely been poisoned by the same thing.

Now that we know exactly what caused the problem, seafood can be checked for domoic acid to make sure there are no more poisonings. Scientists continue to work to understand why these algae grow to high concentrations at certain times, so that we can predict these events, or perhaps even prevent them from happening in the future.

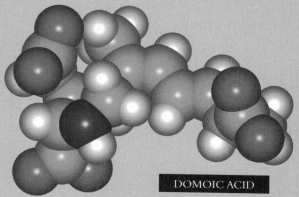

DOMOIC ACID

©M.A. Quilliam, National Research Council Canada

LEAVES AND

Try this trick with a friend or family member.

1 Mash up the dry leaves into little bits and mix it with the dirt in one of the bowls. Place half this mixture into the other bowl.

2 Ask your friend or family member if they would like to have a contest to see who can separate the dirt and leaves the fastest. Have another friend time the contest.

3 Start the clock! While your friend is frantically trying to separate the dirt and leaves, calmly pour water into the bowl. The dry leaves will float to the top, and the dirt will sink.

4 Scoop the leaves out onto a plate. Pour off the water and scoop the dirt onto another plate. Ta dah! You're the winner! Are there any other materials you could do this with? What properties would each material need to have for this trick to work?

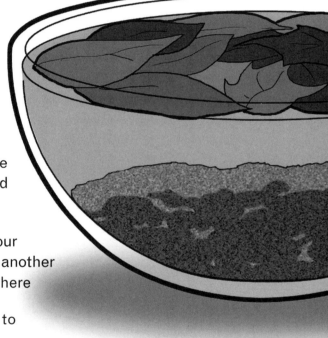

+SuppLies

- dry leaves or sawdust
- dirt
- two deep bowls
- water
- two plates

DIRT TRICK

What's Happening?

The leaves and dirt are a mixture. They can be easily separated because they have different properties. The leaves are less dense than water and they float, and the dirt is more dense than water and it sinks.

When scientists—like you—are trying to figure out what's in something, they first separate a mixture into its different parts. Then each part of the mixture can be tested to see what's in it. Mixtures can be separated by differences in their parts, such as size, density, magnetism, and the temperature at which a material freezes or evaporates. How would you separate marbles from sand? (Hint: how do you separate spaghetti from the water it was boiled in?)

OUTSMARTING BABA YAGA

There are many folktales from Russia about a witch, Baba Yaga. In one version, a young girl, Vasilisa, finds herself in Baba Yaga's clutches, and Baba Yaga gives her three seemingly impossible tasks to perform. If Vasilisa can't do the tasks, Baba Yaga's frogs will eat her! One of the tasks is to separate a huge pile of poppy seeds from dirt, all in one night. Fortunately, Vasilisa has the help of her magical doll, who easily separates the poppy seeds from dirt. Do you think the doll might have used the "magic" of chemistry?

Make Your Own
CHROMA-COLOR

+Supp[L]ies

- scissors
- coffee filters or blotting paper
- several nonpermanent markers of different, dark colors
- cellophane tape
- pencil
- tall glass
- water
- cardstock or construction paper
- hole punch

1 Cut the coffee filter or blotting paper into as large a rectangle as possible. Mark dashed lines 1 inch (2 1/2 centimeters) from the bottom of the paper using a different color marker for each dash.

2 Lightly tape the top of the paper rectangle to the middle of the pencil. Place the pencil on the top of the glass so that the filter paper hangs down inside the glass.

3 Slowly fill the glass with water until the bottom of the paper is in the water, but the dashed lines are out of the water.

4 Let the paper sit for 15 minutes, checking it several times. When the water has spread to the top of the paper, take it out of the water and let it dry.

5 If your colors all ended up near the top, you can repeat steps 2–4, but take the paper out of the water sooner.

6 Cut out two pieces of cardstock so that they are a little larger than your filter paper. Using the hole punch, punch holes through both pieces of cardstock at the same time. Make as many or as few holes as you like, but don't make them too close to the edge. You can make the holes in a design or just place them randomly.

7 Place the filter paper between the cardstock pieces and tape the sides. You now have a stained glass bookmark!

BOOKMARK

What's Happening?

The colors in the markers are a mixture of different colors, or pigments. Our eyes see the pigments as one color because the pigment molecules are completely mixed together and we can't distinguish one molecule from another. But just as the molecules of each pigment have a different color, they have other characteristics that are different too, such as their size and how well they cling to water. The smaller molecules cling to water more, so they travel farther along the paper before attaching to the paper. Looking at your paper, which pigments do you think have larger molecules?

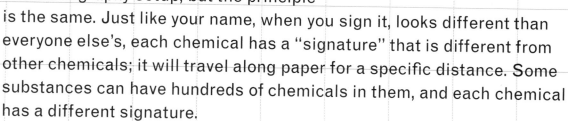

Scientists use different types of chromatography as one way to figure out exactly what is in a substance. They use equipment that is more precise than your chromatography setup, but the principle is the same. Just like your name, when you sign it, looks different than everyone else's, each chemical has a "signature" that is different from other chemicals; it will travel along paper for a specific distance. Some substances can have hundreds of chemicals in them, and each chemical has a different signature.

GET YOUR IRON

1 Put one cup of cereal in the bowl. Mash the cereal with the spoon. Add water to cover the cereal and continue mashing until the cereal is mushy.

2 Swish the magnet through the cereal, especially along the bottom of the bowl. Iron is heavier than water, so it will sink to the bottom. The longer you swish the magnet, the more iron you will collect.

3 Try variations in the experiment to see how you can get the most iron out of the cereal. What happens if you don't mash up the cereal first? What happens if you don't use water? What happens if you wet the cereal with vinegar? Can you think of any other variations? Be sure to use the same amount of cereal to start with each time, and only try one variation at a time so you can see which ones allow you to extract the greatest amount of iron.

+Supp[L]ies

- **breakfast cereal fortified with iron**
- **bowl**
- **spoon**
- **water**
- **magnet**

What's Happening?

Cereal is a mixture of many materials, one of which is iron. Mashing and wetting the cereal breaks up these different materials. Iron can then be easily separated out of the cereal because it is the only substance here that is magnetic.

Iron is an essential nutrient for our bodies. It is used to make hemoglobin in our blood. (Remember when we talked about hemoglobin in chapter 1?) It's easier for our bodies to digest the iron if the cereal is first mashed up, which happens when we chew, and then made wet from our saliva and stomach acids.

Have you ever watched a candle burn? Then you've seen a **chemical reaction**. This is when something changes into something else. Reactions are the heart of chemistry. They may seem like magic, but reactions, like everything in chemistry, happen for a reason.

Reactions
Presto-Change-o!

In a chemical reaction, atoms are rearranged to make a new chemical substance. The materials you start with are called **reactants**, and the materials you end with are called **products**. For a reaction to occur, the bonds in molecules must be broken and new bonds formed. Atoms bond to form molecules by trading or sharing electrons, so when a reaction occurs, electrons are moving around.

Imagine again the room full of people wearing white shirts and black shirts—white atoms and black atoms—that we talked about in chapter 2. The atoms lock arms and form bonds, creating molecules, only now they are in pairs of white–white and black–black. Every time a white–white molecule and a black–black molecule collide, they break their bonds, and the white atoms and black atoms form new bonds by locking arms. This is like the bonds breaking in reactants and new bonds forming to make a new kind of product. After all the molecules have had a chance to collide, the new white–black molecules would be the only type of molecule in the room. This new molecule would have different properties. Maybe it would be a gray molecule!

EXAMPLES OF REACTIONS

Here are some examples of reactions you might see or know about around you:

- nail rusting
- candle burning
- plants using energy from the sun to change water and carbon dioxide into food and oxygen, in a process called photosynthesis
- silver tarnishing
- yeast rising in bread

Sometimes it looks like a material has undergone a reaction, but it hasn't. When water freezes or boils, it's just changing from a liquid to a solid or gas. It's still the same molecule—H_2O. When chocolate melts in your hand, it's not reacting, it's just changing from a solid to a liquid—the mixture is still the same. To learn more about these kinds of changes, see chapter 8, A Change of State.

FULLY RISEN, AND READY FOR THE OVEN!

What Makes Reactions Take Place?

Not all molecules react when they come into contact with each other. Whether an atom bonds with another atom—and how strong that bond is—depends on the number and arrangement of its electrons and how well they match up with the other atom's electrons. To see why, we have to go back to the structure of the atom from chapter 1. Atoms have protons and neutrons clumped together in the nucleus, with electrons orbiting around the outside. Electrons move in shells, or regions of space, arranged a little bit like the rings of an onion. There are up to seven shells around the nucleus, with each holding a certain number of electrons. The innermost, or first, shell can hold 1 or 2 electrons, the second shell can hold up to 8 electrons, the third shell can hold up to 18 electrons, and so on. The innermost shells are always filled up before electrons are added to outer shells.

It's this outer shell that determines whether an atom will bond with another atom. Atoms are the most stable when their outer shell is full.

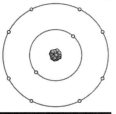

NEON with a stable, full outer shell.

AIRBAGS: INSTANT PILLOW

Ever wonder how a giant pillow of air can come shooting out of such a small space in your car? Because of a chemical reaction, of course—actually, a whole string of them. An unused airbag has different chemicals in it, which are ignited by an electrical impulse that is triggered when the car stops very suddenly. One of these chemicals is sodium azide. Once ignited, sodium azide decomposes, or breaks down, into sodium and nitrogen gas. The nitrogen gas, which takes up more space, quickly fills the airbag.

If the outer shell is full, an atom does not bond easily with another atom. But if the outer shell is one or two electrons short of being full, the atom is unstable. It will react easily by grabbing an electron from somewhere else. Where will the atom find an extra electron? From an atom that has just one electron in its outer shell, which is also unstable. When an atom gets rid of that extra electron hanging in a shell by itself, the shell underneath, which is full, becomes the outermost shell and it is then stable.

Look at the **periodic table of elements.** Use the caption to figure out how to read the chart. Hydrogen, with a symbol of H, is number one in the upper left-hand corner. It has one proton and one electron, and it's in Group 1. (This group used to be called Group I.) Elements in Group 1 have an electron sitting out all by itself in the outermost shell, which isn't stable. These atoms easily give up that electron, leaving a stable shell underneath, or they share it with another atom. Now look on the right side of the periodic table at oxygen, with a symbol of O and an **atomic number** of eight. It's in Group 16 (also called Group VI.) All of the elements in Group 16 have an outermost shell that's almost full; they're just missing two electrons. These atoms like to form bonds where they can grab or share two electrons from other atoms. If one oxygen atom, which needs two electrons, and two hydrogen atoms, each of which wants to give up one electron, bond together, they'll both be happy. Which is exactly what happens when water forms—H_2O.

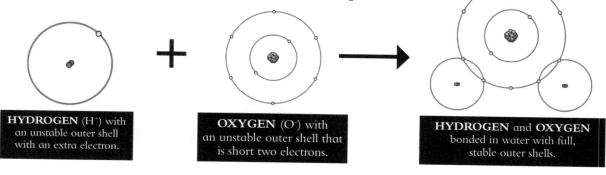

HYDROGEN (H^+) with an unstable outer shell with an extra electron.

OXYGEN (O^-) with an unstable outer shell that is short two electrons.

HYDROGEN and **OXYGEN** bonded in water with full, stable outer shells.

27

WORDS TO KNOW

chemical reaction: the rearrangement of atoms in a substance to make a new chemical substance.

reactants: the substances that are being changed in a chemical reaction.

products: the new substances formed from a chemical reaction.

periodic table of elements: a table that arranges all of the elements according to their properties.

atomic number: the number of protons in the nucleus of an atom. The atomic number is used to distinguish elements in the periodic table of elements.

The Periodic Table of Elements

The periodic table arranges the elements in a way that shows many of their properties and relationships to each other. The horizontal rows are called periods, and the vertical columns are called groups. The groups, numbered 1 through 18, are listed at the top of each column; right underneath in parentheses are former Roman numeral group names I through VIII that are sometimes still used. Each element is represented by a letter symbol, with the full name printed at the top. The atomic number, which is the number of protons in the nucleus, is written above each element.

1 (I)	2 (II)	3	4	5	6	7	8	9	10	11	12	13 (III)	14 (IV)	15 (V)	16 (VI)	17 (VII)	18 (VIII)
hydrogen 1 **H** 1.0079																	helium 2 **He** 4.0026
lithium 3 **Li** 6.941	beryllium 4 **Be** 9.0122											boron 5 **B** 10.811	carbon 6 **C** 12.011	nitrogen 7 **N** 14.007	oxygen 8 **O** 15.999	fluorine 9 **F** 18.998	neon 10 **Ne** 20.180
sodium 11 **Na** 22.990	magnesium 12 **Mg** 24.305											aluminium 13 **Al** 26.982	silicon 14 **Si** 28.086	phosphorus 15 **P** 30.974	sulfur 16 **S** 32.065	chlorine 17 **Cl** 35.453	argon 18 **Ar** 39.948
potassium 19 **K** 39.098	calcium 20 **Ca** 40.078	scandium 21 **Sc** 44.956	titanium 22 **Ti** 47.867	vanadium 23 **V** 50.942	chromium 24 **Cr** 51.996	manganese 25 **Mn** 54.938	iron 26 **Fe** 55.845	cobalt 27 **Co** 58.933	nickel 28 **Ni** 58.693	copper 29 **Cu** 63.546	zinc 30 **Zn** 65.39	gallium 31 **Ga** 69.723	germanium 32 **Ge** 72.61	arsenic 33 **As** 74.922	selenium 34 **Se** 78.96	bromine 35 **Br** 79.904	krypton 36 **Kr** 83.80
rubidium 37 **Rb** 85.468	strontium 38 **Sr** 87.62	yttrium 39 **Y** 88.906	zirconium 40 **Zr** 91.224	niobium 41 **Nb** 92.906	molybdenum 42 **Mo** 95.94	technetium 43 **Tc** [98]	ruthenium 44 **Ru** 101.07	rhodium 45 **Rh** 102.91	palladium 46 **Pd** 106.42	silver 47 **Ag** 107.87	cadmium 48 **Cd** 112.41	indium 49 **In** 114.82	tin 50 **Sn** 118.71	antimony 51 **Sb** 121.76	tellurium 52 **Te** 127.60	iodine 53 **I** 126.90	xenon 54 **Xe** 131.29
caesium 55 **Cs** 132.91	barium 56 **Ba** 137.33	57-70 ✳	lutetium 71 **Lu** 174.97	hafnium 72 **Hf** 178.49	tantalum 73 **Ta** 180.95	tungsten 74 **W** 183.84	rhenium 75 **Re** 186.21	osmium 76 **Os** 190.23	iridium 77 **Ir** 192.22	platinum 78 **Pt** 195.08	gold 79 **Au** 196.97	mercury 80 **Hg** 200.59	thallium 81 **Tl** 204.38	lead 82 **Pb** 207.2	bismuth 83 **Bi** 208.98	polonium 84 **Po** [209]	astatine 85 **At** [210]	radon 86 **Rn** [222]
francium 87 **Fr** [223]	radium 88 **Ra** [226]	89-102 ✳✳	lawrencium 103 **Lr** [262]	rutherfordium 104 **Rf** [261]	dubnium 105 **Db** [262]	seaborgium 106 **Sg** [266]	bohrium 107 **Bh** [264]	hassium 108 **Hs** [269]	meitnerium 109 **Mt** [268]	ununnilium 110 **Uun** [271]	unununium 111 **Uuu** [272]	ununbium 112 **Uub** [277]	ununquadium 114 **Uuq** [289]				

	lanthanum 57 **La** 138.91	cerium 58 **Ce** 140.12	praseodymium 59 **Pr** 140.91	neodymium 60 **Nd** 144.24	promethium 61 **Pm** [145]	samarium 62 **Sm** 150.36	europium 63 **Eu** 151.96	gadolinium 64 **Gd** 157.25	terbium 65 **Tb** 158.93	dysprosium 66 **Dy** 162.50	holmium 67 **Ho** 164.93	erbium 68 **Er** 167.26	thulium 69 **Tm** 168.93	ytterbium 70 **Yb** 173.04
✳ Lanthanide series														
✳✳ Actinide series	actinium 89 **Ac** [227]	thorium 90 **Th** 232.04	protactinium 91 **Pa** 231.04	uranium 92 **U** 238.03	neptunium 93 **Np** [237]	plutonium 94 **Pu** [244]	americium 95 **Am** [243]	curium 96 **Cm** [247]	berkelium 97 **Bk** [247]	californium 98 **Cf** [251]	einsteinium 99 **Es** [252]	fermium 100 **Fm** [257]	mendelevium 101 **Md** [258]	nobelium 102 **No** [259]

RUBIDIUM

Rubidium (Rb) is a soft, silvery metal that is highly reactive—that means it reacts easily with many elements. How reactive? It will burst into violent flames when exposed to water (burning is a reaction), creating an explosion of hydrogen gas. It will even spontaneously catch fire in air because of the water vapor in air. Like other elements in its group in the periodic table of elements, it has one lone electron in its outermost shell. You would think that any element that will set water on fire would react with anything. Strange as it sounds, rubidium is sometimes stored in kerosene, which is quite flammable. But kerosene doesn't react with rubidium because it doesn't want that extra electron in the outer shell.

Fast and Slow

Some reactions happen very fast. Other reactions happen very slowly. A nail rusting reacts too slowly to watch it happen, especially in a dry climate. (To find out why a humid or dry climate might be important, try the rusty shapes experiment at the end of this chapter.)

What makes a reaction go faster? For a reaction to occur, the reactants have to physically come into contact with each other. In our imaginary room of white and black molecules, each molecule has to bump into another before the bonds break and reform. Anything that makes the reactants come into contact more often will increase how fast the reaction happens.

What makes molecules come into contact more often? Higher temperatures, for one. High temperatures make molecules move faster, so they'll be more likely to bump into each other. Another factor is the size of the particles of reactants. Powders, for example, will react faster than a big hunk of a reactant. That's because powders have a much larger surface area, which means there's more area that can come into contact with the

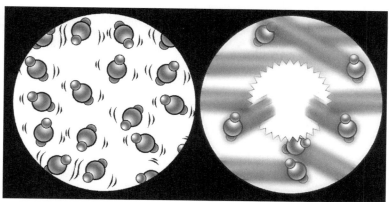

other reactants. Have you ever stirred something before baking it? You're helping to mix together the molecules, which makes the reaction go faster.

HOT AND HOTTER

Some reactions are extremely exothermic; they produce a lot of energy. Explosives are materials that, once ignited, burn very fast, releasing lots of energy and producing a huge amount of hot gas. An explosive has molecules with weak bonds. A little bit of energy, like lighting a match, ignites the explosive and breaks those bonds; that's the **activation energy** discussed below. The atoms rearrange themselves and form stronger bonds and, in the process, release lots of energy.

An explosive is unstable because the molecules are packed together tightly, so it doesn't take much to break some of the bonds. When the bonds break, the molecules fly apart, becoming a gas and releasing lots of energy. The hot gas expands, taking up as much as 1,000 times the volume as the solid or liquid explosive did. All that expanding gas and released energy makes a giant pressure wave, which can explode whatever is around it. The reaction happens so quickly—almost instantly—that the pressure acts as a shockwave traveling through the material. This process is called a detonation.

Fortunately, explosives have an activation energy, so it takes some energy to get the reaction started. Usually, what starts the reaction is heat, but it can be a physical shock for especially sensitive explosives like liquid nitroglycerin.

Dynamite is probably the best known explosive. Dynamite is composed of either wood pulp or **diatomaceous earth** soaked in nitroglycerin and pressed into a stick shape. Nitroglycerin is very unstable—it can explode if it is disturbed—so the wood pulp helps to stabilize the dynamite.

Energy

Reactions involve changes in energy. Some reactions *give off* energy, usually in the form of heat, and they're called exothermic. Combustion, or burning, is the best example of an **exothermic reaction**. If you stand next to a bonfire, there's no doubt that the reaction of wood and oxygen is giving off energy. Most reactions are exothermic.

Endothermic reactions *absorb* energy, or heat. When baking soda and vinegar react, the reaction absorbs energy, and you can measure that by taking the temperature before and after the reaction. Photosynthesis is another endothermic reaction; plants absorb

AHHH... THAT'S THE STUFF!

energy to make the reaction happen. Do you know where plants get the energy for photosynthesis?

It's Hard to Get Started

Have you ever come inside on a hot day and flopped down on the sofa, feeling like a wet noodle? Then a friend calls you to go to the swimming pool, and you'd like to go, but first you have to get off the sofa. You gobble an energy bar and manage to stand up. Once you're up and moving, though, it's easy to keep moving, and soon you're racing to the pool. All you needed was a little boost of energy to get you going.

Most reactions need a little boost to get going. You know that a log of wood can burn. But it needs a boost of energy or heat, like a match, to get it started. Once it catches fire, the log will burn by itself. That extra energy that's needed to get a reaction started is called the activation energy. It's a good thing most reactions need activation energy or things would start burning all by themselves!

Some reactions are spontaneous. A spontaneous reaction doesn't need anything to get it started, it just happens. Rust is a good example. As long as all the chemical reactants are present, iron will rust without any activation energy.

LOOKS TO ME LIKE YOU GOTS A RUST PROBLEM.

I CAN FIX IT, BUT IT'S GONNA COST YA.

WORDS TO KNOW

activation energy: the energy that starts a chemical reaction.

diatomaceous earth: a light material that comes from diatom (fossilized) remains of algae. It is non-reactive.

exothermic reaction: a chemical reaction that releases energy, usually in the form of heat. An example is a burning log.

endothermic reaction: a chemical reaction that absorbs energy. An example is photosynthesis in plants, which absorbs energy from the sun.

corrode: the wearing away of metal by a chemical reaction. Rust is a type of corrosion.

Make Your Own
ALKA-SELTZER ROCKET

Part 1

Caution: Never point the film canister at someone once you have closed the lid. Keep your own face away from the lid. Wear goggles to protect your eyes. Also, Alka-Seltzer contains aspirin. Don't eat it and keep it away from small children and pets. Do this activity outside!

1 Fill the film canister about half full with warm water. You should have your goggles on. Add half an Alka-Seltzer tablet to the water with one hand. With the other, quickly snap on the canister lid.

2 Place the canister on a hard surface, outside, with the lid facing up. Stand back and count how long it takes for the lid to pop off.

3 Try this again and vary the amount of water and Alka-Seltzer or the temperature of the water. Remember to only change one thing at a time. What makes the best rocket?

Tips if you're having trouble:
If your lid is not exploding off, it is probably because the lid on the canister is not tight enough. Try using a film canister that has a lid that fits inside, not one that fits around the outside of the canister. You can also try using another container that has a lid that fits snugly but doesn't screw on, such as the lid on some antacid tablets.

+Supp[L]ies

- eye goggles
- 3 or more film canisters with lids that snap inside, usually clear or white, available free anywhere that develops photos
- water
- several Alka-Seltzer tablets, original formula, from the drugstore
- heavy paper or cardstock
- markers
- sturdy tape, such as masking tape

Part 2

Once you get the hang of popping the lids, try making a rocket. It works best if you have at least one friend to help. And remember, everyone needs goggles.

1 Decorate the paper for the outside of your rocket. Tape the bottom parts of three film canisters together. Tape the long edge of the decorated paper to the film canisters so that the short edge of the paper is even with the openings of the canisters. Wrap the paper around the canisters and tape the other long edge so it overlaps the paper.

2 Cut a circle of paper about 3 inches (7.5 centimeters) in diameter. Make a cut to the center of the circle and overlap the edges to form a cone, and tape the cone closed. Tape the cone to the end of the paper cylinder away from the canisters.

3 Hold the rocket upside down and fill the canisters half full with warm water. Break the Alka-Seltzer tablets in half. With a friend, add half a tablet to each canister at the same time, then quickly snap on the lids.

4 Quickly put the rocket on the ground with the lid side down. Stand back! Do you remember how many seconds it took for the lid to pop off? Start your countdown!

What's Happening?

The Alka-Seltzer tablet is a mixture of baking soda, citric acid, and some other ingredients. In the presence of water, the baking soda and citric acid (the reactants) react to form new substances—carbon dioxide and sodium citrate (the products). That means the molecules in the tablet are breaking apart and forming new ones. Some of the atoms from each substance come together to form a new type of molecule.

One of the new types of molecules formed is carbon dioxide, which is a gas at room temperature. As more and more of the gas molecules are made, they build up pressure inside the canister. (You'll learn more about gas pressure in chapter 7.) It's like more and more people piling into a closet to hide—pretty soon, there will be too many and they'll burst out of the door. The carbon dioxide gas puts more and more pressure on all sides of the canister, and the lid pops off because it has less resistance than the sides of the canister.

Make Your Own
RUSTY SHAPES

1 Pour water into three of the jars, about half full. Add about a tablespoon (15 milliliters) of salt to one of the jars with water and stir. Label the jar.

2 Wash the steel wool with detergent to remove any oil coating. Divide the steel wool pad into fourths. Pull each piece into a different shape, such as a star, a triangle, or an animal. Put one shape into each jar. If necessary, add more water to cover the steel wool in the jars with water. Use a paper towel to dry the steel wool that goes into the jar with air only.

3 Slowly pour a layer of cooking oil about a half-inch thick (1 centimeter) over the plain water in one of the jars. The oil will settle on the top.

4 Take the temperature of each piece of steel wool by inserting the thermometer into the middle of the steel wool for a minute. Record the temperatures, noting whether the steel wool measured was dry, under plain water, under salt water, or under water and oil.

5 Observe the jars a few hours later. Do you see any change in the color of the steel wool? Record the temperatures of each piece of steel wool again and compare them with the beginning temperatures. Have any of them changed?

6 Observe the jars a day later. Do you see more changes? Which jar has changed the most? Which has changed the least? You can keep the experiment going as long as you like, or pull out the shapes and attach them to a thread to make an ornament.

+Supp☐ies

- water
- four glass jars
- salt
- plain steel wool, without a detergent coating
- detergent
- paper towel
- cooking oil
- thermometer (optional)
- embroidery thread (optional)

34

What's Happening?

Iron and steel (which contains iron) rust in the presence of oxygen and water. Rusting is an exothermic chemical reaction, where metal is worn away. The iron atoms in the metal are worn away, or **corrode**, and bond with oxygen atoms to form iron oxide, or rust. When atoms bond, they are transferring electrons. The water acts as a bridge to transfer the electrons. When the steel wool is under water alone, it seems as if it's only exposed to water and not oxygen. But there is oxygen dissolved in the water. That might sound strange at first, but think about how oxygen gets to all parts of our body. First, we breathe air into our lungs. But then the oxygen is dissolved in our blood to be carried to the rest of our body. Fish also breathe oxygen that is dissolved in water.

Only a certain amount of oxygen can dissolve in water at a time. The oxygen in the water reacts with the steel wool and forms a bit of rust—not enough to see at first. As the oxygen is used up, more oxygen from the air dissolves in the water. It's like a bathtub with the faucet on and the drain open; as water leaves through the drain, more is pouring in from the faucet.

Why doesn't the steel wool that's under water and oil rust? Oxygen doesn't dissolve in oil, so when the oil covers the water, it blocks more oxygen from dissolving in the water. Once the small amount of oxygen that's in the water to begin with is used up in the rust-forming reaction, it's gone. Without oxygen, the reaction can't keep going.

You probably saw the most corrosion, or rust, in the steel wool under the salt water. Salt is composed of sodium (Na) and chloride (Cl), with a formula of NaCl. When it dissolves in water, it separates into ions. Remember from chapter 1, an ion is an atom that has either gained or lost an electron and, thus, is either positively or negatively charged. Salt water is water that has lots of positive ions (Na^+) and negative ions (Cl^-) in it. These ions act like an even better bridge than plain water, allowing the flow of electrons to happen faster. The faster the electrons flow, the faster the corrosion happens. Salt water corrodes iron about 10 times faster than air. You probably didn't see any rust on the steel wool in the jar with only air. That steel wool would eventually rust, because there is moisture in the air, but it happens much more slowly.

If you took the temperature before and after the experiment, you probably observed a rise in temperature. That's because rusting is an exothermic reaction, which means that energy is released as a result of the reaction. In this case, the energy is released as heat, so the temperature rises.

CLEAN PENNIES!

1 Pour vinegar into each bowl, enough to cover the bottom. Add about a spoonful of salt to each bowl and stir well. Place half of the pennies into one bowl, and half into the other, keeping out one penny. Hold the extra penny halfway in the vinegar for about a minute. Can you see the difference in the two halves of the penny?

2 Insert a toothpick through the holes of the brass washers and nuts, alternating the washers and nuts. Dip the toothpick into one of the bowls so that the washers and nuts are half in the vinegar/salt solution and half in the air.

3 After about 10 minutes, look at the pennies in each bowl. Do the pennies look different? Take out the pennies from the bowl without the toothpick. Place half of the pennies on the paper towels, and rinse the other half in water before placing them on the paper towels. Label the paper towels.

4 After about a day or two, take out the rest of the pennies, washers, and nuts. As before, put half of the objects on the paper towel to dry, and gently rinse the other half in water first.

5 After the objects are dry, look at them closely. Did your washers, nuts, and pennies change color? Where do you think the color came from? Is there a difference between pennies dated 1982 and earlier, which are solid copper, and newer pennies, which just have a coating of copper?

6 Cut the embroidery thread to about 18 inches (46 centimeters) long. String the washers and nuts on the thread, alternating one washer and one nut. Tie the thread in a knot. You can also use washers and nuts that were not placed in the solution for a silver-color contrast.

+Supp[L]ies

- vinegar
- two bowls
- spoon
- salt
- at least 10 pennies, including some from 1982 and before
- toothpicks
- brass washers
- brass nuts
- water
- paper towels
- embroidery thread

COOL NECKLACE!

What's Happening?

There are lots of things going on in this experiment. Pennies are either made of or coated with copper, a pure substance that is very shiny. But over time, the copper atoms on pennies combine with oxygen atoms in the air to form copper oxide, which gives pennies a dull look. When you place the pennies in a vinegar and salt solution, the vinegar dissolves the copper oxide. Vinegar is a weak acid and doesn't dissolve the copper oxide very quickly, but it has help. The salt breaks down into sodium and chloride ions, and the chloride ions attack the copper oxide. Once the dull copper oxide is dissolved, the copper left behind is shiny.

The pennies that are rinsed begin the slow process of forming copper oxide again, and will turn a dull brown over time. The pennies that aren't rinsed still have vinegar and salt on them. These pennies develop a bluish-green coating, or patina. It is a complex patina of copper chloride.

When the vinegar and salt solution dissolves the copper oxide, some of the copper dissolves too. When the copper atoms leave the penny to go in the solution, they leave electrons behind, so the copper is a positive ion. The washers and nuts are made of brass, which is a mixture of copper and zinc. These copper and zinc atoms also go into the solution as positive ions. So now the pennies and brass washers and nuts have a slightly negative charge. The positive copper ions are attracted to the negative brass surface. Some of those copper ions leave the solution and coat the surface of the brass objects.

DID YOU KNOW?

The Statue of Liberty contains 179,000 pounds (81,000 kilos) of copper, about as thick as the width of two pennies. The green patina on the statue has formed from the copper reacting with the atmosphere. The copper patina, sometimes called verdigris, actually protects the statue from further corrosion, though, because it provides a barrier between the pure copper and the atmosphere.

E ver take a big bite out of a lemon? Try to do it without puckering your lips. That sour taste comes from the **acid** in the lemon juice. Acids can be found in other fruits as well, like limes, oranges, grapes, and apples. The acids in these fruits and many other foods are weak acids and help give foods flavor, but strong acids, such as battery acid, are dangerous and can damage your skin and tissues.

Acids & Bases

The opposite of an acid is a **base**, or alkali. Weak bases, such as baking soda, taste bitter. Strong bases, such as oven cleaner, are dangerous and should never be tasted.

But what exactly is an acid? An acid is a substance that can release a hydrogen ion. Hydrogen is the element that has one proton and one electron. Hydrogen easily gives up its electron, which is in a shell by itself, and becomes a positively charged ion (H^+).

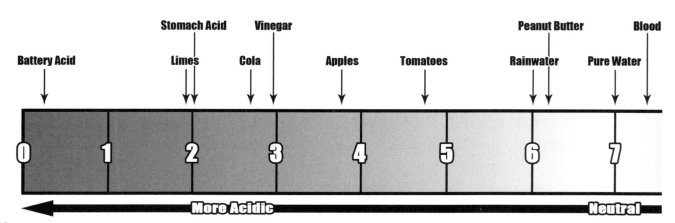

PROPERTIES OF ACIDS AND BASES

Acid	Base
Releases a proton (H^+).	Accepts a proton (H^-).
Corrodes metals.	Breaks apart proteins. Bases feel slippery on your skin because your skin is made largely of proteins and the base is peeling off layers.
Turns litmus paper red.	Turns litmus paper blue.
Tastes sour. (Don't taste anything you don't know is safe!) Try tasting lemon juice or even a little vinegar.	Tastes bitter. (Don't taste anything you don't know is safe!) Put a tiny bit of baking soda on your tongue.
Some acids, from strongly acidic to weakly acidic, are stomach acid, lemon juice, vinegar, sauerkraut, and rainwater.	Some bases, from strongly basic to weakly basic, are toilet-bowl cleaners, limestone, ammonia, antacids, baking soda, and egg whites.

So a hydrogen ion is the same thing as a proton, and you could just as easily say that an acid is a substance that can release a proton.

Since a base is the opposite of an acid, it is any substance that can accept a hydrogen ion (or proton). A base often has what's called a **hydroxyl group**, or (OH^-), because the hydroxyl group will react easily with a hydrogen ion to form water.

These definitions of acids and bases sound very simple. Just one little proton moving around. What's the big deal? That one little proton moving around and reacting has powerful consequences—a strong acid or base can eat through your skin, or even metal.

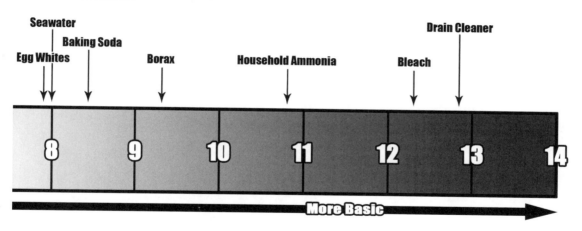

Egg Whites · Seawater · Baking Soda · Borax · Household Ammonia · Bleach · Drain Cleaner

8 · 9 · 10 · 11 · 12 · 13 · 14

More Basic

pH

We measure the acidity or alkalinity of a substance by using the **pH** scale. pH stands for potential of hydrogen, which makes sense because acidity has to do with hydrogen activity. Acids and bases are on opposite sides of the pH scale. An acid has a pH between 0 and 7, and a base has a pH between 7 and 14. A pH of 7 is neutral. The lower the number, the more hydrogen ions there are and the more acidic the substance is. The higher the number, the more basic, or alkaline, the substance is.

pH is measured using an indicator, such as litmus paper. Litmus paper, which comes from lichens, turns red in an acid and blue in a base. Other natural substances, such as turmeric (a spice), blackberries, and red cabbage, can indicate pH.

DON'T PESTER THE GARDENER

Many ants produce **formic acid** that they use in biting or stinging. The acid is part of why an ant bite hurts. In the rain forests of Peru, researchers have discovered ants that use formic acid to "garden." The lemon ants that live there prefer the lemon ant tree because the leaves have hollow stems that provide nest sites for the ants. The ants make sure there are lots of lemon ant trees. They inject formic acid into the leaves of all the plants in an area except the lemon ant tree. The acid causes the leaves to turn brown and fall off in about five days. The lemon ants' "gardening" method makes sure their favorite tree gets lots of sunlight.

Since the pain from an ant bite comes from an acid, it can be neutralized by a weak base to reduce the pain. Which do you think might help make an ant bite feel better, vinegar or baking soda? Look on the pH chart to find out. Bee stings also contain acid, but the pain from a bee sting mostly comes from other substances. Rubbing a weak base on a bee sting probably won't help much, but applying ice will. Ice numbs the pain and slows down blood flow to the area to reduce swelling.

PINK OR BLUE

Hydrangea flowers grow blue or pink, depending on the acidity of the soil they grow in—like litmus paper. Hydrangea flowers can only be blue if aluminum is present in the soil. Most soils contain aluminum, but if the soil is alkaline (basic), the plant can't absorb the aluminum and it won't turn blue. Hydrangea flowers grow pink in highly alkaline soils.

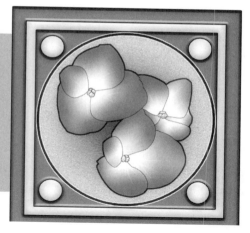

Neutralization

When an acid and a base come together, they react, or change. The acid donates a proton, or hydrogen ion, and the base accepts it. When an acid and a base combine, they form water and a salt. If all the ions from the acid and the base are used up, then the final solution is neutral and the reaction is called a **neutralization**. Sometimes, there is more of either the acid or the base, and not all of the reactants are neutralized. In this case, the final solution has water, a salt, and some of the excess acid or base.

DID YOU KNOW?

Lemon ants get their name because they have a tangy lemony taste—yum!

WORDS TO KNOW

acid: a substance that donates a hydrogen ion (H^+) to another substance. Examples include vinegar and lemon juice.

base: a substance that accepts a hydrogen ion (H^+) from another substance. Examples include baking soda, ammonia, and oven cleaner.

hydroxyl group: an (OH^-) ion, often found in bases.

pH: a measure of how acidic or basic a substance is. The pH measures how many hydrogen ions are in a substance and ranges from 0 to 14.

formic acid: a liquid acid found in and produced by ants and many plants.

neutralization: a reaction between an acid and a base that uses up all the acid and base. The products of the reaction are water and a salt and have a neutral pH of seven.

Make Your Own FOAMY

1 Fill the bottle half full with warm water. Use the funnel to add three tablespoons (45 milliliters) of baking soda.

2 Add a squirt of dish soap. Hold your hand over the top of the bottle and shake it to get the liquid foamy.

3 Add several drops of red food coloring and two drops of yellow food coloring, or any other color you'd like.

4 Set the bottle on the tray. Quickly mold the modeling clay around the bottle into a cone. Adjust the cone to make it level with the bottle opening, but don't block the opening.

5 Use the funnel to quickly pour vinegar into the bottle, just below the rim. Remove the funnel and watch your volcano erupt!

+Supp[L]ies

- **empty wide-mouthed, short, plastic bottle, such as from juice or a sports drink**
- **water**
- **stiff paper or funnel**
- **tablespoon**
- **baking soda**
- **dish soap**
- **red and yellow food coloring**
- **tray or baking pan**
- **modeling clay**
- **vinegar**

AN ACID WORTH ITS

Gold has been valued since prehistoric times. It is beautiful, easily shaped, does not corrode, and hardly anything reacts with it. When the Nazis came to power in Germany in the 1930s, they confiscated gold, especially from the Jewish people. Some Jews tried to smuggle their gold out of the country, including two Nobel Prize winners, Max von Laue and James Franck. They sent their Nobel Prize medals, which were gold, to another Nobel Prize winner, Niels Bohr, in Copenhagen, Denmark.

When the Nazis invaded Denmark in 1940, Niels wanted to protect the medals. But how? He didn't want to bury them because they could always be found and dug up. The Nazis made sending gold out of the country illegal, and the medals had the names of the Nobel Prize winners on them, so if they were discovered, James and Max would be imprisoned, or worse. A scientist named George de Hevesy helped solved the problem. George was a chemist who later won a Nobel Prize for his work in chemistry.

VOLCANO

~~~~~~~~~~~~~~~~~~~~~~~~~~~~~~~~~~~~~

What's Happening?

Baking soda is a base, and vinegar contains acetic acid. When an acid and a base get together, they react and form water and a salt and sometimes other products as well. Baking soda and acetic acid react to form water, sodium acetate (a salt), and carbon dioxide. The carbon dioxide is a gas, which gives the reaction its fizzy bubbles. The dish detergent helps to keep the carbon dioxide bubbles around longer. Gas takes up more volume than liquid, so the products come bubbling out of the bottle. Try making this with green food coloring and a spooky clay shape. Pair it with the Double, Double, Toil and Trouble project in chapter 6 for Halloween fun!

~~~~~~~~~~~~~~~~~~~~~~~~~~~~~~~~~~~~~

WEIGHT IN GOLD

As the Nazis marched into Copenhagen, George dissolved the medals in one of the few things that will dissolve gold: aqua regia (royal water), which is a combination of nitric and hydrochloric acid. The Nazis occupied the place where George worked, and though they were in power—temporary power, that is—they weren't nearly as smart as the scientists. They never found the gold, even though they carefully searched the building. It sat on a shelf the entire time, completely dissolved in the acid, right under their noses. When the war was over, the scientists precipitated the gold out of the acid solution—that means they used another chemical reaction to get the gold out. The Nobel Foundation recast the medals and presented them back to the scientists.

Make Your Own
NAKED EGGS

1 Place your eggs in the bowl. Try to keep the eggs from touching each other. Fill the bowl with enough vinegar to cover the eggs.

2 Set the bowl where you can see it but it will be undisturbed. You can cover it if the vinegar smell bothers you.

3 After at least a day, carefully take out the eggs. They should be soft and the outside may look translucent, so that you can see through them a bit. If the eggs aren't soft, pour out the old vinegar, put the eggs back in the bowl, and cover with new vinegar for another day or so. You may also see a chalky white layer on the outside; if the egg is soft, you can gently rub off this remnant of the shell under running water.

4 Hold your naked eggs a few inches (centimeters) above the kitchen sink and then drop them. How high can you drop an egg before it breaks? Can you gently squeeze your egg?

5 Try doing the same experiment with hard-boiled eggs. (Get an adult to help you boil the eggs.) Are there any differences?

+SuppLies

- a few whole eggs, still in their shells
- bowl
- vinegar

44

What's Happening?

Eggshells are made mostly of calcium carbonate. The egg actually grows the mineral shell. Calcium carbonate is a base, and its chemical symbol is $CaCO_3$. Vinegar contains water and acetic acid, which gives vinegar its sour taste. Acetic acid has a chemical formula of CH_3COOH. All acids have one or more hydrogen atoms (H) because an acid is a hydrogen ion donor. When the vinegar and eggshell come into contact, they react and neutralize each other.

The vinegar dissolves the shell, but did the shell actually disappear? No. The calcium carbonate molecules that make up the shell break up in the reaction and form new molecules, or products. The products of the reaction are carbon dioxide, calcium acetate, and water. The calcium acetate and water are in the vinegar solution, and the carbon dioxide is a gas; it makes bubbles on the surface of the eggs.

Under the shell, the egg is encased in a thin membrane. This membrane becomes rubbery because it allows liquid to pass through it. That extra liquid, plus the flexible membrane, lets you bounce the egg. Watch out, though. If you bounce it too hard—splat!

AMAZING EGGS

A chicken egg is only one cell. Even though the shell feels very hard, it's also permeable, which means that it lets stuff—like moisture, air, and even bacteria—pass through it. The eggshell is about 94 percent calcium carbonate in the form of the mineral calcite. We take the egg for granted, but it's pretty amazing that the egg inside grows something as strong and as uniformly shaped as an egg!

CORALS REEFS: ONE BIG EGGSHELL

Eggshells are mostly calcium carbonate. Seashells, pearls, limestone, and chalk are also made of calcium carbonate. So are some of the most beautiful and complex places on earth—coral reefs.

Animals called corals build coral reefs. Corals take calcium and carbonate ions in seawater and make calcium carbonate skeletons. The ocean is naturally basic, with a pH a little above eight. When the pH is lowered, even if it's still somewhat basic, there aren't as many carbonate ions floating around and it's harder for corals to make their skeletons. When there aren't enough raw materials, the corals can't work efficiently.

What can lower the pH of an entire ocean? An acid, of course. The earth's atmosphere naturally contains a small amount of carbon dioxide. Carbon dioxide in the atmosphere isn't an acid, but when it dissolves in water, it makes a weak acid called carbonic acid. Burning fossil fuels releases more carbon dioxide into the atmosphere to dissolve in water.

The pH of shallow waters in the ocean before the Industrial Revolution was about 8.15; the pH is now about 8.05. That's a small change, but it's enough to mean that there are lower concentrations of carbonate ions. Corals can still make their skeletons, but it's more difficult and they now are more sensitive to other stresses, like pollution. The ocean will never become as acidic as the vinegar in your experiment dissolving the eggshell, but it may not always be basic enough for corals. Scientists are researching the complex interactions between the atmosphere, the ocean, and coral reefs so we can work to make sure corals have what they need to live and grow.

NICE PLACE YOU'VE GOT HERE!

AIN'T BAD, 'CEPT FOR ALL THE TOURISTS!

Make Your Own
INVISIBLE MESSAGES

1 Mix a few spoonfuls of baking soda with the same amount of water and stir. Use a paintbrush or cotton swab to write on the paper with the baking soda solution. Let dry.

2 Using another paintbrush or swab, brush grape juice concentrate over the paper. The writing should show up in a different color.

3 You can also make the writing show by holding the paper up to a heat source, such as a lightbulb. Get an adult to help with this, and don't hold it near a halogen bulb. The writing should turn brown.

+Supp L ies

- baking soda
- water
- paper
- two paintbrushes or several cotton swabs
- grape juice concentrate
- heat source, such as a lightbulb (optional)

What's Happening?

The baking soda solution is virtually invisible by itself, but when it comes into contact with the grape juice, it reacts and turns color. Baking soda is a base, and grape juice is an acid, so this is an acid-base reaction. When you heat the writing, the baking soda is actually burning; it burns at a lower temperature than the paper and turns brown.

DID YOU KNOW?

When he was a general, George Washington often received secret messages from his rebel army. Invisible messages were written between the lines of a regular message in case the British intercepted the letter. General Washington would heat the letter by holding it near a candle flame to reveal the invisible message. Sometimes, he would reveal the message using a chemical agent. The materials used for writing and revealing the invisible messages were different from the ones you have used, but the basic concepts are the same.

Everybody knows what a **solid** is. It's hard, doesn't change its shape, and you can't pour it. But what about a piece of soft fabric? Or a handful of sand? They're solids too. If you look at a small enough piece, like a grain of sand, you can see that it holds its shape. Sand only pours because you have lots of little solid grains. And while fleece might feel soft, that's because the fabric is flexible. It bends, but it's still solid.

Solids
They're Really Not That Hard

To understand what makes something a solid, you have to look at the smallest parts—the atoms. The particles in solids are bound tightly into a particular shape. The atoms can still vibrate, a bit like a string on a violin vibrates, but they can't change places with each other. Because the atoms in solids stay in the same place, solids hold their shape and don't flow to fit a container. If you take a basketball and place it in a bucket, the basketball doesn't change its shape.

Solids can have all sorts of different properties, such as strength, hardness, elasticity, or the ability to bend. Solids have less energy than liquids, which have less energy than gases. Like everything else, those properties aren't "magical" but are there because of the arrangement of the atoms in a solid.

DID YOU KNOW?
Quartz, diamond, sand, salt, and metal are crystalline solids.

When a solid is heated, the atoms vibrate faster and faster, with more and more energy. Once the vibration is too much, the atoms break away from each other. This is called the melting point, and when this happens, the solid becomes the subject of the next chapter—liquids!

WORDS TO KNOW

solid: one of the three states of matter where the particles are bound tightly into a particular shape. A solid has a definite shape and volume and does not flow.

state of matter: the form that matter takes. There are three common states of matter: solid, liquid, and gas.

crystal: a solid where the atoms are arranged in a highly ordered pattern.

geometric arrangements: crystal systems, or ways in which crystals are arranged. There are seven geometric arrangements.

amorphous solid: a solid where the atoms are in a mostly random, but still tightly bonded, arrangement.

pitch: a substance that is made from tar.

viscosity: the resistance to flow of a fluid. A liquid that is very viscous, such as honey, flows slowly.

solute: the dissolved substance in a solution.

STATE OF MATTER

Matter has three common states: solid, liquid, and gas. There are also some far less common states, like plasma, where the electrons are separated from their atoms. The **state of matter** affects the properties of the material, like whether something flows or its density. The state doesn't affect the chemical makeup of the matter, though. For example, water can be a liquid, a solid (ice), or a gas (water vapor or steam). In all three cases, it's still H_2O molecules; the only difference is how those molecules are arranged.

WATER, WATER EVERYWHERE...

...AND NOT A DROP TO DRINK!

DID YOU KNOW?

Some time ago, a gas company needed to ship pitch from England to Spain and loaded broken, apparently solid pieces of it straight into the hold, or bottom, of a ship without first putting it in containers. During the trip, the ship ran into very hot weather, and the pitch didn't stay "solid." All of it melted into a sticky mess, filling all of the nooks and crannies of the ship's hold before it resolidified when colder weather came. When the ship's captain got to his destination, the hold was one solid piece of pitch. If you've ever left a candle on something hot or in the sun on a hot day, you've probably experienced much the same thing.

49

Crystals

Crystals are a special form of solid, where the atoms are arranged in an orderly pattern. If you think of an entire crystal as a building, then the building blocks would be molecules. These building blocks are stacked up like bricks. If conditions are right, the building blocks keep stacking up over and over into a crystal big enough to see.

If you could shrink down to the size of an atom, you would see the regular arrangement of the atoms. But, in fact, you don't have to shrink down to see this; the shape of the big crystal is the same as the shape of the smaller, molecular building blocks.

Often, a solid is made up of many very small crystals packed together in a mass. In this case, the solid doesn't look like a crystal; it will have a rough surface.

There are only seven different types of crystal systems, or **geometric arrangements**, but there are many types of crystals. What makes the difference are the different atoms in each crystal. Blue sapphires and red rubies are the same kind of crystal, but sapphires have small amounts of iron and titanium and rubies have small amounts of chromium.

DID YOU KNOW?

Most plastics, tires, wood, fabric, and paper are solids that are both crystalline and amorphous.

SALTY HOTEL

The Salt Palace and Spa in Bolivia is the world's only hotel made of salt. The walls are made of 14-inch by 14-inch (36-centimeter) salt blocks, cemented together with a saltwater solution. The walls, roof, and floors are salt. Even the tables and chairs are made of salt! The hotel was built in 1993 and sits in the middle of the Uyuni Salt Flats. Salt flats are exactly that: a huge flat area of salt. Long ago, the area was a lake, and as the water in the lake evaporated over time, the salt was left behind. Now, the salt is mined and used as table salt. Maybe some of the salt you used for dinner last night came from the Uyuni Salt Flats.

SALT MARCH

In the 1920s, the British ruled India, but the people of India wanted to rule themselves. Mahatma Gandhi led the struggle for independence, and he used nonviolent action to do so. His most famous action was the Salt March.

People who live in warm climates near the ocean can "make" their own salt. They transfer seawater to shallow pools. The water evaporates, leaving the salt behind. People who lived along the coast of India during British rule made their own salt by evaporating seawater, until the British made it illegal to do so. Instead of collecting and using salt for free, people had to buy it from the colonial government and they had to pay taxes on the salt. It was especially hard for the poor. On March 12, 1930, Gandhi began marching 240 miles (386 kilometers) from Sabarmati to the sea at Dandi, and thousands of people joined him. When he arrived at the coast, he encouraged the people to exercise their freedom and make their own salt. Many thousands did. Seventeen years later, after many more nonviolent actions, the British left India, and the Indian people gained their independence.

GANDHI DURING THE SALT MARCH, MARCH 1930.

Amor...what?

Look out your window. You're looking through an **amorphous solid**—glass. Amorphous solids are the opposite of crystal solids. "Amorphous" means without a definite structure, or disorganized. If you're a messy person, then your room probably has an amorphous appearance. If you think of a crystal as having particles arranged like eggs in a carton all lined up, then an amorphous solid would be like having particles arranged like marbles in a jar—a big jumble. The particles are arranged randomly, like in a liquid, but they're still tightly bound; they can't change places or flow around each other. The plastic in sandwich bags is an amorphous solid, but the best example is the one you see every day—glass.

Amorphous solids can form from liquids that cool very quickly, such as when hot lava cools into volcanic glass. As a liquid cools, the molecules lose energy and move more and more slowly. As the liquid turns into a solid, the molecules normally settle into an orderly arrangement, or crystal. But if the liquid cools very quickly, the atoms do not have time to arrange themselves and they bond in a more random arrangement.

Many solids are a combination of crystalline and amorphous. Wood, for example, has areas that have an orderly arrangement of atoms and other areas where the atoms are randomly arranged.

IS GLASS REALLY A SOLID?

You may have heard somewhere that glass is really a liquid that flows very, very slowly. The main "support" for this is window glass in old cathedrals and other buildings from the Middle Ages that seems to have deformed, or flowed, over time. The glass is often thicker at the bottom of the window. It turns out, though, that the glass was probably uneven when it was made because of the glassmaking techniques at the time. Glass made now is very even in thickness, and experiments don't show glass flowing, even over long periods of time. In fact, glass made during the ancient Roman era hasn't deformed over many centuries.

Most scientists think of glass as an amorphous solid. Just to confuse matters, though, glass does have some properties of liquids, mainly its random arrangement of atoms, so there are some scientists who think of glass as its own state of matter, neither liquid nor solid.

DID YOU KNOW?
Window glass, raw rubber, volcanic glass, wax, and fulgurites (glass that forms when lightning strikes sand) are amorphous solids.

GOING, GOING...STILL GOING...

Have you ever done an experiment that seemed to take forever? Perhaps you had to boil water or grow mold and you had to wait many long minutes, or maybe even days. In 1927, at the University of Queensland in Australia, Professor Thomas Parnell started what is listed in the Guinness Book of Records as the longest-running laboratory experiment. He wanted to prove that something that seems to be a solid can have liquid properties if you wait long enough, and he used pitch to do it. Pitch is a substance made from tar and is very similar to it, but **pitch** is more solid than tar. At room temperature, it looks and feels like a glassy rock and can be shattered by a hammer blow.

Thomas heated the pitch to make it flow and poured it into a sealed funnel. He let it cool and settle for three years, then took off the seal. Not much happened for a very long time—eight years, in fact. Although pitch looks like a solid, it flows like a liquid, but very, very slowly. That's because it is extremely **viscous** (viscosity is a measure of how fast something flows)—100 billion times more viscous than water. It took all of those eight years for one single drop to fall through the funnel into the beaker below. As of today, 80 years later, only a total of eight drops have fallen. Drops are taking even longer to fall now because air conditioning was installed in the building, which cools the pitch and makes it even more viscous.

If you ever visit the University of Queensland, be sure to visit Professor John Mainstone, the current caretaker of the experiment, at the Department of Physics, where the Pitch Drop Experiment is on display. The experiment will probably run for at least another 100 years, so you have plenty of time. Maybe you'll actually see a drop fall. If you do, you'll be the very first one, because it only takes about a tenth of a second for the drop to fall, with eight or more years in between drops. Blink and you'll miss it!

Make Your Own CRYSTALS

Caution: This project involves boiling water, so get an adult to help.

To form a crystal, you will mimic how crystals are formed naturally. If a hot liquid is cooled slowly and not disturbed, the crystal can form slowly and grow larger. A small disturbance can make the liquid turn solid too quickly, though, making lots of very small crystals, or even an amorphous solid without a crystal structure.

Place a few salt grains onto black paper or a dark surface and look at the grains closely, using a magnifying glass if you have one. What shape are the grains? You'll compare this salt to the crystals you grow.

Tips for Making Crystals
- Let your crystals grow where they won't be disturbed.
- The longer you wait, the larger the crystals will grow.
- Use distilled water or rainwater, especially if you have "hard" water.
- Try different mixtures to see what works best!

+SuppLies

- **table salt (sodium chloride)**
- **black paper**
- **magnifying glass (optional)**
- **cotton string**
- **saucepan**
- **water**
- **teaspoon**
- **long-handled spoon**
- **food coloring (optional)**
- **shallow pan**
- **glass jar**
- **paper towels**

1 Cut the string into about eight pieces, each about 6 inches (15 centimeters) long. Tie the strings together at one end. Boil about 2 cups (473 milliliters) of water in the saucepan. (Make sure you have an adult for this part).

2 Stir in salt slowly, one teaspoon (5 milliliters) at a time. Mix well each time. Continue adding salt until it starts to collect on the bottom of the pot. If you want colored crystals, add food coloring.

3 Allow to cool for a minute, then carefully pour about half of the solution into the shallow pan and the other half into the jar. Do not allow any of the undissolved salt to get into the jar or pan.

4 Place the strings into the jar, with the knotted end submerged in the salt solution. Let the other ends drape over the rim of the jar.

5 Move the pan and jar to a location out of the light where they will not be disturbed. Place paper towels under the jar to catch any drips from the strings. Leave the solution for about two weeks, checking each day. If the level of the solution goes below the knot, add more salt solution, prepared as above.

6 The salt crystals should start forming in about a day. The slower the crystals grow, the larger they will be. Look at the crystals closely. How are they different from the original salt crystals? How are they the same? Do the crystals forming in the pan look different from the ones on the strings? Try the same experiment with different lengths of string, in different arrangements or shapes. Can you make a string salt sculpture?

What's Happening?

Table salt, or sodium chloride, is a crystal solid, which means that the sodium and chloride atoms are arranged in order. When you add salt to water, it goes into solution, which means the sodium and chloride atoms separate and are surrounded by water molecules. Water can hold only certain amounts of a **solute** such as salt before it won't dissolve anymore. The solution is saturated at this point. But hot water can hold more salt than cold water can, so when the water cools, it's holding more salt than normal. If it cools slowly and isn't disturbed, the salt can form fairly big crystals.

Grow Lots Of
NEEDLE-LIKE CRYSTALS

Place a few Epsom salt grains on the black paper and look at them closely. What shape are the grains?

1 Cut the paper into whatever shape you like, such as a snowflake or heart. Place the paper on the cookie sheet. Cut the paper if it doesn't fit completely within.

2 Slowly pour the Epsom salts into the hot water, stirring constantly. Keep stirring until all of the Epsom salts are dissolved, if possible. Add food coloring if you like.

3 Pour the solution over the paper. Place the cookie sheet with the paper and solution in a warm place, like a sunny window. With an adult's help, you can also place the cookie sheet in a warm oven (200 degrees Fahrenheit/93 degrees Celsius) for 15 minutes or so, but watch it to make sure it doesn't dry out too much. You should start to see lots of large, spiky crystals growing. How are they different from the original, Epsom salt crystals?

+Supp[L]ies

- black cardstock or construction paper
- 1 cup (236 milliliters) Epsom salts from the pharmacy
- scissors
- short-sided cookie sheet, or pie pan
- 1 cup (236 milliliters) hot tap water
- food coloring (optional)
- magnifying glass (optional)

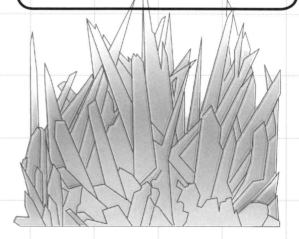

DID YOU KNOW?
Epsom salts are used for healing cuts and shallow wounds. The mineral epsomite, which is the same as Epsom salt, was first discovered near Epsom, England. Epsomite can be found encrusting limestone cave walls.

Make Your Own
ROCK CANDY

Caution: Make sure you have an adult to help with the cooking.

Place a few sugar crystals onto a sheet of black paper or dark surface and look at the grains closely, using a magnifying glass if you have one. What shape are the grains?

1 Tie one end of the string to the button and wrap the other end around the pencil. Put the pencil over the glass so that the string hangs down into the glass. Adjust the length of string so that the button is just above the bottom of the glass.

2 Pour about 1 cup (236 milliliters) of water into a saucepan and add the sugar. Heat the sugar-water mixture until it boils, stirring until the sugar dissolves or the syrup has small bubbles in it. (Make sure you have an adult for this part).

3 Cook the sugar syrup over medium heat for 3 minutes without stirring. Remove the saucepan from the heat and let cool for 2 minutes. Carefully pour the syrup into the glass to just below the rim. If there is extra sugar on the bottom of the saucepan, do not let it flow into the glass.

4 Using a potholder, move the glass to a warm place where it can be easily seen but will not be disturbed.

5 Be patient! Watch the crystal grow each day, but wait for at least a week before touching the glass. The longer you wait, the bigger the sugar crystal will grow. What shape are the crystals?

6 If no crystal forms, or if the whole glass of syrup turns into a solid lump, you may have stirred it while it was boiling. Try again!

+Supp[L]ies

- black paper
- sugar, about 2 cups (473 milliliters)
- cotton string
- button
- pencil
- glass or tall jar
- water
- saucepan
- potholder
- food coloring (optional)
- magnifying glass (optional)

Make Your Own
CANDY-GLASS HOUSE

Caution: This project involves very hot liquids, so get an adult to help.

1 Cut the milk containers in half lengthwise. Tape the ends so you have six shallow rectangular containers. If you have more than three containers, you can use the extra pieces for decorations. Completely coat the inside of the containers with the cooking spray.

2 Put the sugar in the saucepan. Heat the sugar on low to medium until it turns brown and melts. Be patient— it will take about 10 minutes. As soon as the sugar melts completely, get an adult to help you pour it into the containers. Tilt the containers to coat the bottoms with syrup. Be very careful– the sugar is very hot.

3 Place the containers in the refrigerator or freezer and let them cool on a level surface. When the syrup has hardened, carefully cut the corners of the cardboard and pull the cardboard away from the sugar glass. You should have four or more rectangles of sugar glass. Look carefully at your sugar glass. Do you see any crystals?

4 Use icing to "glue" the edges of the sugar glass panes together to form a box. Add any edible confections, like gumdrops or marshmallows. If you have broken pieces of "glass," make extra decorations like a chimney or bush.

+Supp[L]ies

- scissors
- 3 or more pint-size (473 milliliters) empty cardboard milk containers, rinsed out and dried
- cellophane or masking tape
- cooking spray
- 2 cups (473 milliliters) sugar
- potholder
- icing
- edible decorations
- magnifying glass (optional)

What's Happening

Look carefully at some pieces of sugar and at your sugar glass house. Sugar is a crystal. The sugar you buy from a store has fairly small crystals; if you made rock candy in the experiment above, the crystals were much larger. The rock candy crystals had a long time to grow into very ordered crystal shapes. You cooled the candy-glass house so quickly the liquid sugar didn't have time to form crystals. It's not perfectly clean glass, because reactions while you're heating the sugar give it a brown color.

W hat shape is water? Or milk? The answer: whatever container you put it in, of course. Liquids take the shape of their container. They flow because clusters of molecules can slide past each other. Molecules in a liquid have more energy than those in a solid but less than those in a gas.

Liquids
Go With the Flow!

In some liquids, the molecules find it harder to slide past each other. These liquids are more viscous, which means, as you may recall from the Pitch Drop Experiment in chapter 5, that they have more resistance to flow. Try pouring water into one glass and corn syrup or honey into another. Which takes longer? The corn syrup is more viscous—sometimes we say that it is "thicker." Viscosity is important in industrial processes, like refining and using oil.

Water **Honey**

DID YOU KNOW?

When a liquid is pushed on by a force, the pressure from that force is the same throughout the liquid. This law is called **Pascal's principle**, and it also applies to gases.

Density

Density is the amount of **mass** in a certain **volume**. In general, solids are slightly denser than liquids (but see chapter 10 for an exception), and liquids are a lot denser than gases. Different liquids can have slightly different densities, depending on their chemical makeup.

Density increases by either adding more mass (molecules) to the same amount of volume or by making the volume that the molecules are in smaller. The opposite decreases density. If you add salt to water, the salt breaks apart and its particles slip into the spaces between the water molecules. The mass increases, but because the salt particles slipped into empty spaces, the volume doesn't increase, so salt water is denser than plain water.

Heating a liquid makes it a bit less dense. With heating, the molecules move around faster, so there's a little more space between the molecules. The same number of molecules in a slightly larger volume means the liquid is less dense. The same principles of density apply to solids and gases as well.

WEAKER MOLECULAR BONDS, KNOWN AS HYDROGEN BONDS, BREAK AND REFORM EASILY IN LIQUID WATER.

Hyrdogen Bond = • • • • •   Breaking Bond = ◯

THIS ALLOWS THE MOLECULES TO SLIDE OVER EACH OTHER AND FLOW.

LIKE CHANGING PARTNERS IN A SQUARE DANCE!

NOW DO-SA-DO YOUR MOLECULE!

WORDS TO KNOW

Pascal's principle: when a liquid or gas is pushed on by a force, it transmits the force to all parts of the fluid.

density: the amount of matter in a given space, or mass divided by volume.

mass: the amount of matter or "stuff" in something. On Earth, the mass of something is very close to its weight.

volume: the amount of space occupied by something.

displace: to move or take the place of.

Archimedes's principle: when an object is placed in a fluid, it experiences an upward force that is equal to the weight of the fluid that is displaced.

BEN FRANKLIN'S OIL

A MINUTE ON THE LIPS...

...FOREVER ON THE SHIPS!

Benjamin Franklin was a great inventor and diplomat, as well as one of America's founding fathers. He was also a very curious person, which made him an excellent scientist. In 1757, when he was on a ship in a fleet traveling to America from England, he noticed that the ships at the end of the line had smoother sailing than those in front. Of course he wondered why. The ship's captain gave him a clue when he said, "The cooks have been just emptying their greasy water through the scuppers, which has greased the sides of those ships [at the end] a little."

Ben remembered that explanation about oil smoothing the water. One windy day, when he was back in London, England, he dropped about a teaspoon of oil into Clapham Pond and watched as it slowly spread out. Oil is less dense than water and floats on top. That little bit of oil kept spreading and spreading until it covered an area about as big as half an acre (an acre is about as big as a football field). Ben said the oil made the water "as smooth as a looking glass."

Over a hundred years later, Lord Rayleigh, a famous scientist, built on Ben's experiments. He determined that when the oil was spread out, it was as thick as one molecule. From there, an estimate of the molecule's size could be calculated.

Floating and Sinking

Have you ever kicked back in a refreshing lake or pool and felt the water lift you up? The water is pushing up against you, supporting some of your weight. What happens when you try to lift your head out of water? You start to sink. Whether something floats or sinks depends on its density. Something that is very dense sinks because it's heavier than the water it **displaces**. Your body is less dense than water, so you float. But when you lift your head up, your body isn't displacing as much water, and you start to sink.

Big, steel ships look like there's no way they could float; after all, they can weigh tens of thousands of tons. But they do float because the weight of the water that the ship hull displaces equals the weight of the ship and the cargo combined. The weight of an object is important, but so is its shape because that's what determines how much water is displaced. By itself, steel is denser than water and sinks, but a ship also has wood and air and people, which together have a lower density than water.

EUREKA!

More than 2,000 years ago, Archimedes, a Greek mathematician and scientist, had a problem to solve. King Hiero, who ruled Syracuse in Greece, had ordered a crown of pure gold from a local goldsmith. When he got the crown, it looked and felt like gold, but King Hiero wasn't sure it was gold. He wondered whether the goldsmith had mixed some of the gold with silver, which was cheaper, and kept the leftover gold for himself. Hiero called upon Archimedes to find out if the goldsmith had cheated him.

Archimedes had to figure out a way to tell if the crown was pure or a mixture of metals without hurting the crown. He knew that if he could find out the exact volume of the crown, he could figure out if it was pure gold. Different materials have different densities, so two different materials that weigh the same would have different volumes. Since the goldsmith had been given a specific weight of gold, the crown should have a specific volume. If the gold was mixed with silver, the crown would have a greater volume because silver is less dense. But how to find out the exact volume of the crown? Archimedes couldn't melt the crown into a cube, which would allow him to use a ruler to measure the exact volume. Finding the volume of something as irregularly shaped as a crown seemed impossible.

The story goes that when Archimedes was bathing, he noticed the water overflowed as he stepped in, and the solution to the crown problem came to him; he could tell the exact volume of the crown by measuring the volume of water it displaced. If the crown was made of silver and gold together, it would displace more water than one made only of gold. He was so excited that he ran naked into the street, yelling, "Eureka!" which means "I've found it!"

Archimedes lowered the crown into a bowl full of water and measured the amount that overflowed. He did the same thing with a cube of pure gold the same size as the one the king had given to the goldsmith. The result? More water overflowed for the crown than for the piece of pure gold. Things didn't look too good for the greedy goldsmith. Archimedes proved that the crown was indeed made of gold and silver.

Archimedes used the experience to develop what has come to be known as **Archimedes's principle.** This principle states that when an object is placed in a fluid, it experiences an upward force that is equal to the weight of the fluid that is displaced. Also known as the principle of buoyancy, it determines whether something sinks or floats.

BUBBLE, BUBBLE, TOIL & TROUBLE

1 Remove any labels from the jar and fill it about two-thirds full with water. Pour in cooking oil to an inch (2.5 centimeters) below the rim. Add a few spoonfuls of salt. Look carefully.

+Supp[L]ies

- clear, large jar, such as a mayonnaise jar
- water
- cooking oil
- salt

What's Happening?

Oil and water don't mix. You may have even heard the saying "They're like oil and water," which means that two people don't get along. Oil is less dense than water, so it normally floats. Salt dissolves in water, but not in oil. When you pour the salt on top of the oil, it sticks to the top of the oil and doesn't dissolve. Undissolved salt is more dense than oil or water, so it sinks, taking blobs of oil with it. At the bottom, the salt slowly dissolves into the water. Without the weight of the salt, the blobs of oil rise again. Try this with green food coloring in a large, clear container for Halloween fun!

Make Your Own
WAVE TANK

1 Remove any labels from the bottle. Fill the bottle half full with water. Add a few drops of blue food coloring and one drop of green food coloring to the water. Add mineral oil.

2 Cut a piece of candle and carve it into whatever shape you like. Drop the candle into the water. Screw on the lid and tilt the bottle from side to side. Try tilting it fast and slow, as well as big tilts and small tilts. How is it different?

What's Happening?

The oil is more viscous—it flows more slowly—than the water and so it slows down the flow of the water. Oil and water don't mix (see chapter 10 to find out why) and oil is less dense than water, so it floats on top. The candle is less dense than the water or oil and floats on the very top.

+SuppLies

- 2-liter clear plastic bottle
- water
- blue and green food coloring
- 1/2 cup (118 milliliters) mineral oil or baby oil
- butter knife
- piece of candle small enough to fit through the bottle opening

DOES IT FLOAT?

1 Fill a bowl with water and drop the objects you've collected into the water. Which ones float? Which sink? Take a chunk of clay and roll it into a ball; drop it into the water. Does it float or sink?

2 Now take the ball of clay, form it into a boat shape, and drop it into the water. Does it float or sink? Try placing some of the other objects into the boat. What does it take to sink the boat?

3 Drop the balloon into the water. What happens? Blow up the balloon, tie it off, and place it in the water. What happens?

+Supp☐ies

- bowl
- water
- various objects, either hollow or solid, such as corks, marbles, leaves, tennis balls, and so on
- clay
- balloon (uninflated)

What's Happening?

Things float if they are less dense than whatever they're floating on. In this case, the objects are floating on or sinking in water. Density is how packed together the molecules are, and air is much less dense than water or solid objects. So hollow objects make the overall density much less.

No matter what shape the clay is in, it weighs the same, but it displaces more water when it is in the shape of a boat. The rubber in a balloon is denser than water, but the combination of rubber and air make the inflated balloon much less dense than water.

Make Your Own
LAYER-CAKE LIQUIDS

1 Cut out a circle of paper, as large as possible. Cut halfway across the circle to the center. Fold the paper circle into a long funnel shape, with the center of the circle being the point of the funnel. Tape the edges and cut off the point of the funnel to make a small hole. Repeat with the other sheets of paper to make three funnels altogether.

2 Pour honey or syrup into the bottom of the jar until it is about a quarter full. Do not let the honey touch the sides of the jar.

3 Pour water into the measuring cup to the one-cup (236 milliliters) mark. Add a few drops of food coloring.

4 Hold one funnel so the tip rests against the side of the jar, just above the honey. Slowly pour in the water until it is the same depth as the honey. Try not to let the liquids mix. If they do, let them set for a minute until they separate.

5 Using cooking oil instead of water, repeat step 4, without using food coloring. Using rubbing alcohol instead of water, repeat step 4, using a different color food coloring.

6 Lower the objects into the liquids, being careful not to disturb the liquids. Which is the densest object? Which is the densest liquid?

+Supp[L]ies

- scissors
- 3 sheets of paper
- tape
- honey or syrup
- tall glass jar
- water
- measuring cup
- food coloring
- cooking oil
- rubbing alcohol
- various objects, such as a grape, piece of candle, marble, raisin, ping-pong ball

What's Happening?

Where the liquids and objects sit depends on their density. If you start at the bottom of the jar and go up, you'll go from most dense to least dense. A grape, for example, is less dense than honey and more dense than water, so it floats right in between those liquids.

DID YOU KNOW?

Have you ever heard the expression "blood is thicker than water"? It means that family is important. But it's also true in another way. Blood is about three times more viscous than water because it has lots of "stuff" in it, like red blood cells and platelets. That's mostly a good thing. But when blood is too viscous, it might not be so good for your heart because it has to pump a lot harder to move the "thicker" blood around your body. The good news is that the same things that help keep your blood thin are good for you in many other ways too: eat healthy foods, get plenty of exercise, and don't smoke.

Make Your Own
OCTOPUS DIVER

1 Very slightly blow up the balloon and hold it closed. Wrap one rubber band around the end several times until the balloon is clamped shut.

2 Copy the octopus shape onto aluminum foil and cut out. Drape the aluminum foil over the balloon and twist the foil around the rubber band; wrap another rubber band on top. This is the head of the octopus. Lightly twist the other aluminum foil parts into "arms" of the octopus.

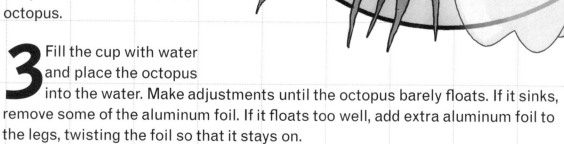

3 Fill the cup with water and place the octopus into the water. Make adjustments until the octopus barely floats. If it sinks, remove some of the aluminum foil. If it floats too well, add extra aluminum foil to the legs, twisting the foil so that it stays on.

4 Fill the bottle with water to overflowing. Put the octopus in, add more water to the brim, and screw on the lid. Squeeze the bottle. What happens?
Try varying the experiment, changing only one thing at a time. What happens if you fill the bottle with salt water? What happens if you change the temperature of the water by adding ice cubes or hot water once the octopus is in the water?

What's Happening?

Air is less dense (heavy) than water or aluminum foil. The air in the balloon makes the octopus float. The molecules in air have a lot more empty space between them, which means it's easier to push the molecules together. When you squeeze the bottle, the pressure you apply transfers to all parts of the water. It's hard to compress water, though, because the molecules are already packed together, so the water transfers the pressure to the air. The molecules in the air are easily pushed closer together, which makes the air more dense, or heavy. Making the balloon smaller also means that your octopus is displacing a smaller volume of water. These two things make the octopus sink. When you let go, the air expands again, and the octopus floats.

FLOATY FISH

Many fish have an organ called a swim bladder; it helps them move up and down in the water without using extra energy. A swim bladder is a pouch that holds gas and works a bit like your octopus. Fish can fill or empty their swim bladder to give them the density they need to float or sink. More gas means they float upwards; less gas means they sink. Fish have a unique ability to move oxygen into or out of their swim bladder from their blood.

Most squid and octopus don't have a swim bladder. But there is one exception. The *Ocythoe tuberculata* is the only octopus that has a swim bladder, and only the females have one. It's also the only kind of octopus that doesn't lay eggs—it gives birth to live young.

+Supp[L]ies

- balloon
- two rubber bands
- aluminum foil
- scissors
- tall cup
- water
- clear plastic wide-mouthed bottle

Some things in this world are invisible, even without a magic spell or invisibility cloak. Blow on your arm. Even though you usually can't see **gases** because they're transparent and colorless, you can see or feel the effects they have. Gases are one of the three states of matter, along with solids and liquids. They're much less structured than the other two; gases easily change both their volume and shape. A gas will not only flow like a liquid, it will also expand to fill a container.

Gases
It's Something In the Air

If you could shrink to the size of a molecule and float around in a gas, you would see mostly . . . nothing. About 99.96 percent of the total volume of gas is empty space. The molecules are very far apart relative to their size, but they have lots of energy. Gas molecules travel in a straight line until they run into another gas molecule or a molecule from the sides of the container they're in. It's like a classroom of kids who have all just eaten lots and lots of candy, bouncing off the walls and each other. Each gas molecule travels at different speeds, but on average gas molecules travel very fast.

DID YOU KNOW?
Oxygen gas molecules on a warm day travel at an average speed of about 1,030 miles (1,658 kilometers) per hour—faster than a jet airplane. Those oxygen molecules don't cross a room very fast, though, because they each have about 5 or 6 billion crashes with other molecules in one second.

HOW NEWTON GOT IT WRONG

Sir Isaac Newton is arguably the greatest scientist who has ever lived. He developed calculus and described the fundamental laws of motion and gravity, among many other discoveries. But even the greatest among us is sometimes wrong. Being wrong occasionally is probably necessary to achieve greatness because it means you're willing to take risks.

Another great scientist who lived around the same time as Isaac, in the seventeenth century, was Robert Boyle. Robert discovered one of the fundamental laws about gases. This law, called Boyle's law, states that when pressure increases on a gas, the volume decreases (as long as the temperature stays the same). If you close the opening of a bicycle pump and press down on the handle, the volume decreases but the pressure increases. It gets harder and harder to push. Robert had discovered the law, but he didn't know why gases acted this way and no one else did either.

Isaac developed a theory about why. He proposed that the particles (or molecules) of air were motionless and were held apart by forces that repelled each other. Pushing on a gas, or applying pressure, was like pushing on a spring. It gets harder and harder as the spring compresses.

Isaac's theory explained the facts beautifully, but it was wrong. Even geniuses have their off days. That's important to remember because there are times when something seems to fit the facts perfectly, but you may not have all of the facts. That was the case for Isaac; no one had all of the facts yet. Later experiments have shown that all molecules are always moving (even molecules in solids move by vibrating) and that they are attracted to each other. The reason the pressure increases when a gas is compressed inside a container is because the molecules crash into a different part of the container much more frequently. When a molecule hits the sides, it exerts a force on the container, and it is the force of all of these crashes that causes gas pressure. When the container gets smaller, there is less surface area for the molecules to crash into, which raises the pressure. The opposite is also true. When the container gets larger there is more surface area for the molecules to crash into, which lowers the pressure.

DID YOU KNOW?

Because gases have so much space between the molecules, gases can be compressed, or squeezed, into a smaller space.

Temperature is a measure of the average speed of molecules. If heat is added, then the average speed increases. Even though gas molecules are very far apart relative to their size, because they move so very fast, they collide a lot with each other.

Those collisions are what cause **gas pressure**. Gas pressure is the force of all of the molecules colliding with the sides of a container. When there are fewer molecules bouncing around and hitting the sides, the pressure is lower. More molecules hitting the sides increases the pressure.

When a Gas is More Than a Gas

Gases are almost always less dense than liquids because the molecules are so far apart. (Density is the mass in a given volume.) As the pressure on a gas increases, it gets denser because the molecules are squeezed closer together. After a certain point, the molecules are so close together that the gas turns into a liquid. But at a very high temperature, called the critical temperature of a gas, the gas won't turn into liquid no matter how high the pressure. At that point it's called a **supercritical fluid**.

You won't find this happening in your fireplace, though. It doesn't have enough heat or high enough pressure. The cores of stars have supercritical fluids, and the planet Jupiter has some gaseous layers that are supercritical and denser than water. Most decaffeinated coffee has its caffeine removed using supercritical carbon dioxide.

DID YOU KNOW?

Tardigrades, also called water bears because they move a bit like a bear, are segmented animals smaller than the head of a pin. They are remarkable creatures. Some species of tardigrades can survive in extremely high or low pressures—as high as 6,000 times as great as our atmosphere, or as low as outer space. They can be found living on top of Mount Everest, at the bottom of the ocean, in the Arctic, at the equator, in hot springs, and probably on some moss or lichen in your own backyard.

POPPING EARS

Have your ears ever "popped" when going up or down quickly in an elevator or airplane? The atmosphere is always pressing on every part of us, and the lower the **elevation**, the greater the atmospheric pressure. We don't usually feel it because air inside our body is pressing out with the same pressure. When you come down quickly from a higher elevation, though, your eardrums feel more pressure from the outside at the lower elevation and they are pushed inward. Your body tries to compensate by balancing the pressure on both sides of the eardrum by allowing some air into the inner ear. You can help by yawning, chewing gum, swallowing, or holding your nose and mouth closed while gently blowing out. This forces air into small tubes that connect the inner ear to the throat.

DID YOU KNOW?

The perfect vacuum doesn't exist. There are always some molecules around—even in outer space. Space comes closest to a vacuum, though, with just a few hydrogen atoms per cubic inch (centimeter) of space. So scientists usually use the term "partial vacuum" instead of "perfect vacuum."

Vacuums

Vroom! A vacuum cleaner works because a pump creates lower gas pressure in the tube. The pressure from the atmosphere stays the same, and it pushes the air (and some dirt along with it) into the vacuum.

You may have heard the phrase "Nature abhors a **vacuum**." It's true, because gases fill whatever container they're in. Imagine you have a container that has a partition in the middle, and the left side has no molecules and the right side has lots of molecules. If you pull out the partition, the molecules that are on the edge of the right side will bounce in every direction. Some of those molecules will bounce towards the left side, but there won't be any molecules to get in their way so they'll keep going until they hit the side of the container. More and more molecules on the right side will do so. Because molecules travel so fast, the vacuum will be filled in an instant.

WHEW!

EXPERIMENTING CAN BE MESSY!

73

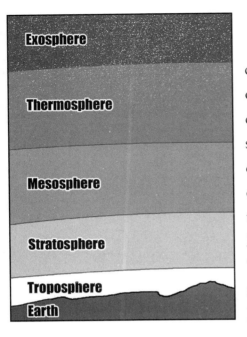

If gases expand to fill any container, why doesn't all of the air leave the earth? Actually, a bit of it does. In the top layer of the **atmosphere**, called the exosphere, some molecules do exit into space. Not very many, though, because the exosphere doesn't have many molecules compared with lower atmospheric layers, and many of those molecules don't have enough energy to escape the pull of gravity. The molecules that do escape are replaced by gases produced by volcanoes. Most air is held closer to the earth because of gravity's pull. The atmosphere slowly gets thinner (that is, fewer molecules) farther from the earth's surface until, at about 600 miles (965 kilometers) high, it merges into space.

THE ATMOSPHERE

The atmosphere is composed of these elements and compounds that are in the gaseous state.

Nitrogen	78.1%	
Oxygen	20.9%	
Argon	0.93%	
Carbon dioxide	0.04%	
Neon	0.002%	
Helium	0.0005%	

Plus, trace amounts of methane, krypton, hydrogen, xenon, nitrogen oxides, sulfur oxides, and water vapor.

Even though water vapor is present only in amounts of 1 percent to 4 percent close to Earth, it is responsible for all our rain and weather.

WORDS TO KNOW

gas: a state of matter where the particles are not bound to each other and move very fast in all directions.

temperature: a measure of the average speed of molecules in a substance.

gas pressure: the force of gas molecules hitting the surface of a container.

supercritical fluid: gas that is at such a high temperature (the critical temperature) that it cannot turn into liquid.

elevation: height above sea level.

vacuum: a space that is empty of matter.

atmostphere: the blanket of air surrounding Earth.

EGG IN A BOTTLE

Caution: This project involves matches, so get an adult to help.

1 Check to make sure the opening to the bottle is slightly smaller than the egg. Large juice or sports drink bottles often work well.

2 Scrunch up the paper and drop it into the bottle. With your adult helper, light the match and drop it into the bottle. Immediately place the egg on top of the bottle opening. Watch!

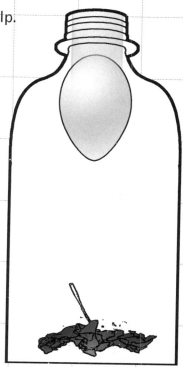

What's Happening?

As the flame burns, it heats the air. Hot air takes up more space than cold air. Where does it go? You may have noticed the egg jumping on top of the bottle. The egg acts as a one-way valve, letting the hot air out of the bottle. But as the flame goes out, the air cools and takes up less space. This makes a partial vacuum, and the pressure from the air outside the bottle pushes the egg into the bottle. Sometimes, people say the pressure changes in the bottle because burning uses up oxygen, but burning also produces carbon dioxide, so it doesn't change the number of molecules or the pressure.

+Supp[L]ies

- **hard-boiled egg, peeled**
- **clear glass or heavy plastic bottle with neck slightly smaller than the egg**
- **paper**
- **matches**

Make Your Own
MENTOS EXPLOSION

1 Roll one of the index cards into a tube as wide as the opening of the bottle. Tape the tube at the top and bottom. Open the bottle of soda and set the bottle on the ground outside; make sure it doesn't tip over.

2 Stack the Mentos in the index-card tube. Place the second index card on top of the tube and turn the tube upside down. Place both on top of the opening of the bottle so that the tube is just over the opening, with the flat index card in between.

3 Pull out the index card and let the Mentos slide into the soda. Stand back!

4 Try some variations. (Remember to only vary one thing at a time.) The fruit variety of Mentos is smoother than the mint; which makes a bigger explosion? Is there a difference between regular and diet soda? Do other candies work as well as Mentos?

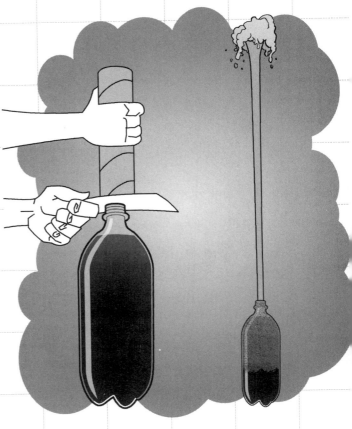

+Supp[L]ies

- two index cards
- cellophane tape
- 2-liter bottle of diet soda
- roll of mint Mentos candy

76

What's Happening?

Big chemical reaction, right? Probably not. That soda whooshing out of the bottle is likely not a chemical reaction at all. A chemical reaction happens when molecules break apart and combine into new ones, and that doesn't seem to be happening here. Changes can come from other physical forces, though.

Soda is bubbly because it contains carbon dioxide—a gas—dissolved in water. That carbon dioxide was dissolved into the soda at the factory under high pressure. Water molecules are strongly attracted to each other (read more about why in chapter 10), and they surround the carbon dioxide, preventing the carbon dioxide molecules from coming together to form bubbles. You can't see the carbon dioxide in a closed bottle, but when you open the bottle, you can see bubbles form and you can feel them fizzing in your mouth when you take a sip. The bubbles form because you have reduced the pressure, and the carbon dioxide comes out of solution.

When you shake the bottle, the carbon dioxide gas molecules can come together and form bubbles. Then, when you open the bottle, the carbon dioxide whooshes out of the bottle and takes some of the soda with it.

The Mentos have a similar effect to shaking a soda bottle. They allow gas bubbles to form. Remember, the carbon dioxide molecules are surrounded by water molecules that trap them. Once a bubble forms, it can grow very quickly; the trick is for the bubble to form in the first place. The surface of an object provides a place where a few carbon dioxide molecules can get together away from the water molecules. Once a few come together, others quickly follow. If you could look at a Mentos candy under a microscope, you would see that its surface is very uneven, with lots of nooks and crannies. These are the perfect place for LOTS of bubbles to form.

This isn't a chemical reaction, where molecules are breaking apart and forming new ones. It's a physical process. The surface of the Mentos candy is simply helping the carbon dioxide gas molecules come together. There may also be some ingredients in the soda and Mentos that help this process as well, but the main factor seems to be the surface of the Mentos. When you drop the Mentos candies into the soda, they fall to the bottom, forming bubbles along the way. The bubbles form very quickly and also rise to the surface very quickly, taking lots of soda with them. Whoosh!

RISING WATER

Caution: This project involves matches, so get an adult to help.

1 Cut a thick slice of the banana or fruit and set it on the pan. Stick the candle into the banana. Pour about an inch (2.5 centimeters) of water into the pan. If you are using a candle that can stand up by itself, like a votive candle, set it directly on the pan.

2 With the assistance of an adult helper, carefully light the candle and place the glass jar upside down over the candle.

3 Watch carefully. Do you see any bubbles? What's happening when the candle goes out? What happens next?

+SuppLies

- **banana or other soft fruit**
- **butter knife**
- **pan or short-sided cookie sheet**
- **small birthday cake or votive candle**
- **water**
- **matches or lighter**
- **glass jar**

What's Happening?

The candle goes out when it has used up the oxygen in the enclosed area. It doesn't change the volume of the gas inside much, though, because the oxygen combines with carbon in the candle to produce carbon dioxide gas. But the air inside is being heated up, and hot air takes up more space than cold air because hot molecules move farther away from each other. You may have seen bubbles right after you covered the candle; this is because the air was heated by the flame. Soon, though, as the hot air hit the colder glass, the air cooled slightly, even before the flame went out. Cooler air takes up less space because the molecules are moving closer together. This creates a partial vacuum because the pressure of the air outside the bottle is greater than the pressure inside the bottle and the air pushes the water up into the bottle. When the candle goes out, the water rises faster because the air is cooling even faster.

SWIMMING RAISINS

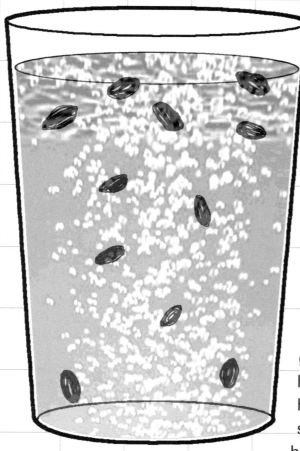

1 Fill the glass about two-thirds full with soda. Put the raisins in the drink and watch what happens.

What's Happening?

The raisins will sink when you first put them in because they are denser than the soda (see chapter 6 for more information on liquids, density, and floating). But after a bit, bubbles start to form on the raisins and they rise. The bubbles are carbon dioxide gas from the soda, and they are less dense than the liquid. Raisins have lots of nooks and crannies, so there are lots of places for bubbles to form—enough to make the raisins rise to the top. Once they're at the top, the bubbles break and the raisins fall back to the bottom—until more bubbles form. How many times do your raisins float and sink? Try this experiment with angel hair pasta to see which works better. Put in food coloring and use this as a fun centerpiece for a party.

+Supp L ies

- tall, clear glass
- clear soda drink from a container just opened
- several raisins

STRETCHY TAFFY

Caution: The taffy syrup gets VERY hot, so get an adult to help, especially when pouring the syrup.

1 Mix together in the pan the sugar, corn syrup, cornstarch, salt, water, and glycerin. Heat over medium heat until the sugar is completely dissolved.

2 Continue stirring until the liquid boils. Cover and let boil without stirring for a few minutes to let any crystals wash down the sides of the pan.

3 Uncover and continue to boil until the syrup reaches the hard-ball stage, or 260 degrees Fahrenheit (125 degrees Celsius), then remove from the heat. When you test the temperature, don't let the candy thermometer touch the bottom of the pan. Using a thermometer is the best way to test the taffy syrup, but you can also drop a small spoonful into a glass of chilled water. When the syrup forms a ball that is rigid but still bendable, the syrup has reached the "hard-ball" stage and is ready.

4 Add the butter, flavorings, and food coloring and stir. Remove the saucepan from the heat. Slowly pour the mixture onto a buttered cookie sheet to cool. Get an adult to help pour, and hold the pan just a few inches (centimeters) above the cookie sheet so that it won't splatter. You can sprinkle nuts, coconut, or small pieces of fruit onto the syrup if you'd like.

+Supp[L]ies

- friend to help pull taffy
- large saucepan with lid
- 2 cups (473 milliliters) sugar
- 1 cup (236 milliliters) light corn syrup
- 1 tablespoon (15 milliliters) cornstarch
- 1½ teaspoons (7 milliliters) salt
- 1½ cups (354 milliliters) water
- 2 teaspoons (10 milliliters) glycerin from a pharmacy or grocery store (optional)
- large spoon
- candy thermometer
- buttered cookie sheet
- 2 tablespoons (30 milliliters) butter plus more for pulling
- 1 teaspoon (5 milliliters) vanilla or peppermint extract or other flavoring, such as cocoa powder
- a few drops food coloring (optional)
- nuts, coconut, or fruit (optional)
- butter knife
- wax paper

80

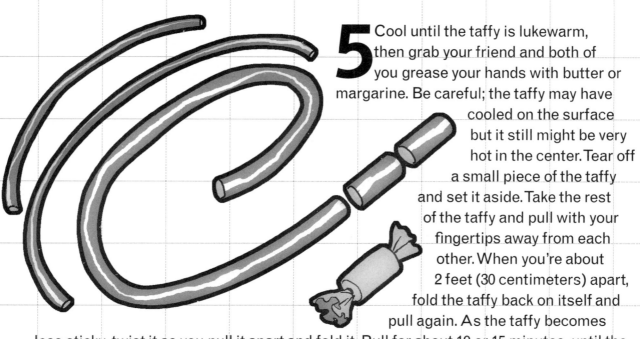

5 Cool until the taffy is lukewarm, then grab your friend and both of you grease your hands with butter or margarine. Be careful; the taffy may have cooled on the surface but it still might be very hot in the center. Tear off a small piece of the taffy and set it aside. Take the rest of the taffy and pull with your fingertips away from each other. When you're about 2 feet (30 centimeters) apart, fold the taffy back on itself and pull again. As the taffy becomes less sticky, twist it as you pull it apart and fold it. Pull for about 10 or 15 minutes, until the ridges from the twisting begin to hold their shape.

6 Pull or roll the taffy into a long rope about ½ to 1 inch (1-2 ½ centimeters) thick. Grease your butter knife, and cut the taffy into whatever size pieces you like. After the taffy is completely cool, wrap the pieces with wax paper, twisting the ends. How does your taffy taste? How does it compare with the small piece you set aside before you pulled and folded the taffy?

DID YOU KNOW?

Modern candy makers use technology to produce about 1,000 pieces of taffy every minute.

What's Happening?

At first glance, this activity doesn't seem to have anything at all to do with a gas. But even though it's not listed, air is a crucial ingredient for making great taffy. If you don't believe that, try eating that little bit of the candy you tore off in step 5 before you pulled the taffy. Every time you stretched and folded the taffy, you trapped tiny air bubbles in the candy. This process is called aerating, and it's used in many baking recipes when you beat or whip the ingredients. These bubbles give taffy its fluffy, chewy texture.

I f you hold a chocolate bar in your hand, after a few minutes you'll have a gooey (but delicious!) mess in your hands. What happened and why? All matter can exist in three different states: solid, liquid, and gas. When a substance changes from one of these states to another, it is called a change of state or **phase change**.

A Change of State

The most important thing to know about phase changes is that they aren't a chemical reaction. When a chocolate bar melts, the bonds *within* molecules are not breaking apart and rearranging the atoms into new molecules, as would happen in a chemical reaction. The change from solid to liquid happens when enough heat is absorbed—in this case, heat from your hand—that the strong bonds *between* the molecules break apart and the molecules can then slide over each other. The molecules themselves don't change, and no new substances are formed. If you take that melted chocolate bar and place it in the refrigerator, it will become a solid (though misshapen) candy bar again. To understand why substances change their state, first we have to take a look at heat.

Heat and Temperature

Heat and **temperature** aren't the same thing. The particles in all substances are in constant motion. In solids, the particles vibrate; in liquids, they slide over one another; and in gases, the particles bounce around at high speed. Temperature is a measure of the average speed at which the particles are moving. At higher temperatures,

DID YOU KNOW?

Heat always flows from hot objects to cold objects. This is known as the second law of thermodynamics. (There are other ways of stating this law, so don't get confused if you hear another version.)

the particles are vibrating or moving faster on average. Temperature is measured with a thermometer. Heat, though, is the total energy of all of the particles in a substance. Believe it or not, a glacier has more heat in it than a bowl of hot soup simply because it's so much bigger and has so many more particles. It has a lower temperature, though, because on average the molecules are moving much more slowly.

This difference is important in phase changes. When a solid turns into a liquid or a liquid turns into a gas, heat is absorbed to make the change. The heat, or energy, goes into breaking the bonds, but the molecules don't move any faster at first, so the temperature doesn't rise during the phase change. This heat is called **latent heat**, which is hidden heat.

Let's look at what happens if you add heat to water in its solid form, ice. All molecules are constantly moving; in solids, like ice, the molecules vibrate. If you add heat to ice, its temperature will rise, which means the molecules vibrate faster and faster. When the molecules are vibrating fast enough (at 32 degrees Fahrenheit/0 degrees Celsius), there's

too much energy, and the bonds between the molecules break. The ice changes to water. Energy is needed to break the bonds, so the temperature doesn't rise while the ice is changing into water. All of the heat goes into breaking the bonds.

When all of the ice has changed to water, the temperature begins to rise again. This means the water molecules, forming clusters that move past each other, move faster and faster. When the molecules are moving fast enough (at 212 degrees Fahrenheit/100 degrees Celsius),

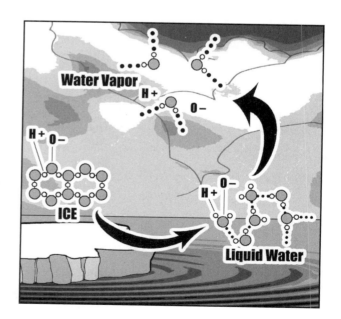

SWAMP COOLERS

In very dry climates, people have used latent heat to help cool buildings. Windcatchers, which are devices that draw hot air across water to cool the air down, have been used for centuries in Persia, now called Iran, and, in fact, are still used there. Evaporative coolers, sometimes called swamp coolers, are used today in hot, dry areas like the desert Southwest of the United States. They pull hot, dry air across filters soaked with water. As the dry air passes through the filters, the water evaporates into the dry air.

Because of latent heat, evaporation draws heat out of the air, cooling it down. Swamp coolers don't work in humid climates because very little of the water evaporates.

The next time you're sweltering hot, try hanging a damp sheet in front of a fan (make sure there's enough space between the two so the sheet doesn't catch on the fan blades) or wrap yourself in the sheet. If anyone asks what you're doing, say that you're harnessing the latent heat of evaporation.

the molecule clusters break apart. The water changes to steam, or **water vapor**. While this change happens, the temperature doesn't rise because all of the heat goes into breaking the bonds. Once all of the water has changed into steam, the temperature begins to rise again as the gaseous molecules move faster and faster.

On a hot day, your body uses this latent heat to cool you down. Your body sweats, and as the sweat evaporates, it absorbs heat from your body. In the reverse, when a gas turns into a liquid or a liquid into a solid, latent heat is released.

Melting Points and Boiling Points

Every substance has a **melting point**, the temperature at which the solid changes to a liquid. This is the same as the freezing point; melting and freezing are really the same process, just in opposite directions. Every substance also has a **boiling point**, the temperature at which the liquid changes to a gas (the opposite is called the condensation point). Solid water (ice) melts to liquid water at about 32 degrees Fahrenheit (0 degrees Celsius), gold melts at 1,947 degrees Fahrenheit (1,064 degrees Celsius), and tungsten (the element with the highest melting point) melts at about 6,192 degrees Fahrenheit (3,422 degrees Celsius). Why do substances melt/freeze and boil/condense at different temperatures?

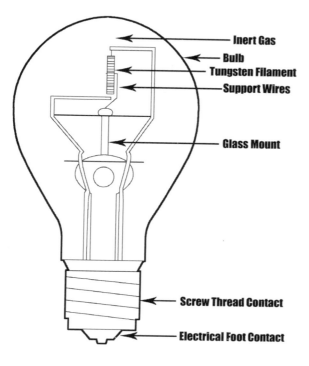

- Inert Gas
- Bulb
- Tungsten Filament
- Support Wires
- Glass Mount
- Screw Thread Contact
- Electrical Foot Contact

DID YOU KNOW?

Tungsten is used in nearly all incandescent light bulbs (the kind used in most lamps) because of its extremely high melting point. A metal must be heated to very high temperatures before it will emit light, and most metals melt before they reach that point.

All matter is made up of particles that are attracted to each other, a bit like magnets. But all these particles are also in constant motion, which pulls the particles apart from each other. You can think of it as two forces that pull in different directions; the attraction pulls the particles together, and the energy from motion pulls them apart. In a solid, the particles are tightly bound because there isn't enough energy from motion to overcome the strong bond of attraction. In a liquid, the particles are in clusters that come together and then move apart because the attraction and energy from motion are about equal in strength. In a gas, the particles bounce around quickly without being bound to each other because the energy from the motion is much greater than the force of attraction pulling them together.

SUBLIMATION

Sometimes a solid turns directly into a gas, without going through the liquid state. This is called **sublimation**, and you can see its effects as close as your nearest freezer. Leave a full ice cube tray in your freezer for a very long time and you'll notice the ice cubes will shrink and eventually disappear. This is because the ice is sublimating, or going directly to a gas. You may have seen sublimation on Halloween. Dry ice, which is frozen carbon dioxide, sublimates to a gas, forming a spooky-looking fog.

Substances have different melting and boiling points because they differ in how strongly their particles are attracted to each other. Tungsten, for example, has a very high melting point because the force of attraction between its atoms is very, very strong. It takes a lot of energy from motion, or a high temperature, to overcome the attractive force and break the bonds so that it melts. Ice, on the other hand, melts to water at a much lower melting point, because the force of attraction between its molecules is not as strong. It takes less energy from motion, or a lower temperature, to overcome the attractive force between the water molecules.

MUHAHAHAAA!!!*

A Fourth State of Matter

There are some other states of matter, although we don't normally encounter them. The best known is **plasma**. In the plasma state, the electrons have been stripped from the atoms, leaving free electrons and bare nuclei (see chapter 1 for an explanation of atoms and electrons). A plasma can be formed either by heating a gas to a very high temperature or by passing an electric current through a gas. The sun forms plasma naturally.

WORDS TO KNOW

phase change: the change from one state of matter—solid, liquid, or gas—to another.

heat: the total energy from the motion of all of the particles in a substance.

temperature: a measure of the average speed of molecules in a substance.

latent heat: the heat that is released or absorbed when a substance changes its state.

water vapor: the gas state of water.

melting point: the temperature at which a solid melts, or turns to a liquid. Different substances have different melting points. (The opposite of a melting point is the freezing point.)

boiling point: the temperature at which a liquid boils, or turns to a gas. Different substances have different boiling points. (The opposite of a boiling point is the condensation point.)

sublimation: the change of a solid directly to a gas without passing through the liquid phase.

plasma: a state of matter under high heat or pressure where the electrons have been stripped away from the nucleus.

supercooling: when a liquid cools below its melting/freezing point without turning to a solid.

PROVING THE IMPOSSIBLE

If you put two containers in a freezer, one filled with hot water and one filled with cold water, which freezes first? The cold one, of course, because water has to be very cold to freeze. In 1963, almost any chemistry or physics teacher would have thought it impossible for the hot container to freeze first.

In 1963, Erasto Mpemba was a schoolboy in Tanzania, Africa. He and his friends loved to make ice cream at their school. They would boil milk, add sugar, let the mixture cool, and then put it in a freezer. The freezer never had enough room for all of the ice cream, so the boys worked quickly to get space in the freezer. One day, Erasto saw the freezer was filling up fast, so he put his ice cream in without cooling it first. When he came back later, his ice cream was ready, but that of another boy, who had put in a cooler ice cream mixture at the same time, was still a thick liquid. Erasto asked his science teacher how this could be, who replied, "You were confused, that cannot happen."

A few years later, Erasto was studying heat in his high school physics class. Erasto asked the teacher how his hot ice cream mixture could have frozen before the cooler mixture. The teacher stated that Erasto was confused. Erasto insisted that he was not confused, and the teacher said, "Well, all I can say is that that is Mpemba's physics and not the universal physics." From then on, whenever Erasto made a mistake, his classmates would say, "That is Mpemba's physics." But Erasto began to experiment with freezing hot and cold water.

Later, a university professor, Dr. Denis Osborne, visited the school, and Erasto told him of his experiments and again asked his question of how hot water can freeze faster than cold water. The professor thought Erasto was mistaken, but he wanted to encourage the students to question things. So he told Erasto, "The facts, as they are given, surprise me because they appear to contradict the physics I know." Erasto continued his experiments, demonstrating to his fellow students and teachers that hot water could indeed freeze faster than cold. Denis also tried the experiment many times and got similar results.

Erasto Mpemba and Denis Osborne published a paper about the unusual effect and proposed some reasons about how it could happen. Although scientists in earlier times had described this effect, modern science had forgotten it until Erasto and Denis rediscovered it. Even today, there is no single explanation that is accepted by all scientists. One proposed reason is that as hot water cools, it evaporates. Evaporation takes away heat very quickly and also reduces the amount of water, which means there is less water to cool. Another reason could be that water can sometimes cool and stay liquid a few degrees below the temperature that water normally turns to ice (32 degrees Fahrenheit/0 degrees Celsius) if it is not disturbed. This is called **supercooling**, and it happens more with water that starts cold than with water that starts hot.

Erasto Mpemba believed what he actually saw happen instead of what everyone expected to happen. Today, the unusual effect of very hot water freezing before cooler water is named for the young student who wouldn't take "impossible" for an answer: the Mpemba effect.

TRY MPEMBA'S EFFECT

Caution: This project involves very hot water, so get an adult to help.

1 Select two or three containers that can hold very hot liquids. Avoid metal containers if possible; ceramics are a good choice. The containers must be the same size and shape because container shape can affect how fast the liquid cools.

2 Clear a space in the freezer that can fit all of the containers. If possible, make a big enough space so that the containers don't touch each other or the freezer walls.

3 With your adult helper, fill a saucepan with water and heat to almost boiling. When the water is close to boiling, run the tap water until the water is as hot as you can get it, but ideally between 140 and 150 degrees Fahrenheit (60-65 degrees Celsius).

+Supp[L]ies

- two or three identical containers
- freezer
- saucepan
- water
- measuring cups
- thermometer
- oven mitts or pot holders

4 Measure one cup (or whatever amount will mostly fill your container) of hot tap water into one container. Quickly measure exactly the same amount of almost boiling water into the second container. If you have a third container, measure the same amount of cold water into it.

5 Immediately place the containers into the freezer using pot holders. Try to avoid having the containers touch each other or the freezer walls.

6 Check your containers every 10 minutes or so to see which container freezes first.

The Mpemba effect works under some conditions but not under others. You can try the experiment again, changing one variable at a time to see what makes a difference. Variables include the size and shape of the containers, whether the containers are heated first, and the location of the containers in the freezer.

What's Happening?

Mpemba's effect, where hot water freezes faster than cooler water under certain conditions, is not completely understood. It probably involves some combination of reasons. As explained in the sidebar on Erasto Mpemba on page 87, one factor might be that as hot water cools, it evaporates. Evaporation is a change of state and it absorbs heat in the process. Evaporation reduces the amount of water, which means there is a smaller amount of water to cool. Another factor could be that water can sometimes cool and stay liquid a few degrees below the temperature that water normally turns to ice (32 degrees Fahrenheit/0 degrees Celsius) if it is not disturbed. This is called supercooling, and it happens more with water that started cold than with water that started hot.

Make your own
VANILLA ICE CREAM

+Supp[L]ies

- **measuring cups and spoons**
- **2, quart-size (liter) zippered plastic bags**
- **1½ cups (354 milliliters) whole milk**
- **1½ cups (354 milliliters) heavy cream, also called whipping cream**
- **3 tablespoons (45 milliliters) sugar**
- **1½ teaspoons (7 milliliters) vanilla**
- **1 gallon-size (3.8 liter) zippered plastic bag (if possible, use a freezer bag)**
- **3 to 4 cups ice**
- **thermometer (optional)**
- **1 cup (236 milliliters) rock salt, or table salt**
- **cloth**
- **sprinkles, fruit, nuts, chocolate sauce, whipped cream (optional)**

1 Pour the milk, cream, sugar, and vanilla into one of the smaller plastic bags and seal. Try not to leave too much air in the bag. Place this bag into the other small bag and seal.

2 Place one cup of ice into the large bag. If you have a thermometer, take the temperature of the ice, then add ½ cup (118 milliliters) salt.

3 Place the small bag in the large bag with the ice. Fill the large bag with the rest of the ice, add the rest of the salt, and seal.

4 Cover the bag with a cloth to protect your hands from the cold. Gently shake the large bag from side to side for about 15 minutes or until the ice cream is solid.

5 Open the large bag and if you have a thermometer, take the temperature of the ice/salt/water mixture. Did the temperature change? Wipe off the top of the small bag, open carefully, and . . . yum! Add any toppings you like. If the ice cream is too soft for your liking, you can put it in the freezer for a few minutes to harden. If you'd like, try this again without the salt. What happens?

What's Happening?

The solid ice cream looks very different from the liquids you added together, but this change isn't because of a chemical reaction. The liquid underwent a change of state, that is, it simply changed from a liquid to a solid. When you started, the molecules in the liquid moved with energy and formed weak bonds with other molecules that easily broke as the liquid moved. When you put the bag in the ice, though, the liquid transferred heat to the ice, because heat always flows from hotter substances to cooler substances. The molecules in the ice cream liquid moved more and more slowly. When they lost enough energy and were moving slowly enough, they formed strong bonds in a crystal structure and became solid.

What about the salt? Salt lowers the melting point of water below 32 degrees Fahrenheit (0 degrees Celsius), which means that water freezes and ice melts at a lower temperature. This is why some of the ice melts when you add the salt. More salt lowers the melting point even more. Salt dissolves in water, separating into sodium and chloride ions. These ions get in the way of the water molecules forming a crystal structure. The whole slushy ice/water/salt mixture is colder than the normal freezing point of water, which allows the ice cream mixture to transfer enough heat to the salty slush so that it freezes, or becomes solid.

DID YOU KNOW?

What's the most popular flavor of ice cream? Black raspberry? Peppermint? They aren't even in the running. Vanilla is the most popular ice cream by a long shot—about 26 percent of all ice cream eaten is vanilla, followed by, you guessed it, chocolate, at about 13 percent.
And, of course, warm states, like those in the South, must eat the most ice cream, right? Wrong again. The top three cities for the quantity of ice cream eaten are Portland, Oregon; St. Louis, Missouri; and Seattle, Washington. Who knew? So does that mean the top month for eating ice cream is January? Nope, it's July, which also happens to be National Ice Cream Month.

Crush a Can
WITH NO HANDS

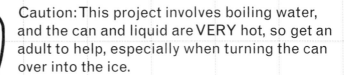

Caution: This project involves boiling water, and the can and liquid are VERY hot, so get an adult to help, especially when turning the can over into the ice.

1 Fill the bowl with ice water and place it next to the stove. Pour enough tap water into the empty soda can to cover the bottom.

2 Cover the bottom of the saucepan with about 2 inches (5 centimeters) of tap water. Put on the oven mitts, and heat the water in the saucepan until boiling. With your adult helper, use the tongs to hold the can in the boiling water.

3 When steam comes out of the can opening, wait one minute, then use the tongs to carefully and quickly flip the can upside down and place immediately in the bowl of ice water. Be careful not to let the boiling water inside the can splash on you. Watch what happens.

+Supp[L]ies

- bowl
- ice
- water
- empty soda can
- saucepan
- oven mitts or pot holders
- tongs

What's Happening?

When the water in the can is heated, it boils and turns into gaseous water, called water vapor. The water vapor pushes out some of the air in the can. When you turn the can upside down into the ice, the water vapor quickly cools down from losing heat to the icy water and surrounding air, and it turns back into liquid water. Liquid water takes up much less space than water vapor, but no air can get in to fill the space, so there is a partial vacuum inside the can. The outside air pressure stays the same. The difference between the outside and inside pressure is greater than the strength of the can, and it is crushed.

Polymers.

You may never have heard of them, but you've seen them. They're all around you. Touch your head; you're touching a polymer—your hair! Polymers are in plastic milk cartons, bicycle helmets, tires, playground balls, cotton, wood, tennis shoes, and your toothbrush.

Poly-Whats-Its?

If it weren't for polymers, you wouldn't be you. Who you are is determined in part by deoxyribonucleic acid, better known as DNA. These are the big molecules in your body that contain coding for all sorts of things, from what color hair you have to whether you are left-handed or right-handed. DNA, along with all proteins, is a polymer.

DID YOU KNOW?

"Poly" comes from a Greek word that means many. "Mono" means one.

Polymers are molecules that are long chains made up of many smaller molecules called **monomers**. How many? Usually, tens of thousands of monomers. If you think of a monomer as a paper clip, then a polymer would be a very long chain of paper clips.

Some polymers are natural, like your hair. Many others, like the plastic milk carton, are synthetic, or manufactured. This kind of plastic is usually made from petroleum, or oil (but polymers are beginning to be made from renewable resources like starch).

DID YOU KNOW?

Kevlar® is a polymer. It's a special kind of fiber that is five times stronger than steel, and it is used to make body armor and sports equipment. Kevlar was first created in 1965 by Stephanie Kwolek. When Stephanie was a young girl, she thought she might want to be a fashion designer. She also loved science, though, and pursued an interest in chemistry. She worked at a company called DuPont, researching high-performance fibers. In a way, she still ended up designing clothing because one of the most important uses of Kevlar is bulletproof vests. Stephanie's invention has saved the lives of more than 2,000 police officers and opened up a whole new field of polymer chemistry. Bulletproof vests are even worn by police dogs. About her work as a chemist, Stephanie has said, "You have to be prepared in chemistry. You have to have a certain background. You have to be inquisitive about things. You have to have an open mind."

How a polymer looks, feels, and behaves has to do with which monomers it's made out of and how those monomers are put together.

A polymer can be hard or soft, rigid or flexible. To make plastic objects, chemists and engineers first make the type of polymer they need based on the properties they're looking for. For example, a bicycle helmet needs a much tougher polymer than a grocery bag. Usually, the polymer is first made into very small pieces, in factories. These pieces are then melted and molded into tubes, sheets, or any other shape desired.

DID YOU KNOW?

Not everything can form polymers. Water, for example, can't link to itself in long chains. The reason monomers can link to other monomers is because of carbon. Carbon has many special characteristics, like the ability to form more than one bond per atom. As a result, carbon can form long chains of polymers, which is also why carbon is the basis of all life. For life to exist, large, complex molecules are needed to store energy, pass on genetic information, and form tissue.

The Adding Game

Many polymers are made simply by one monomer adding onto the end of another over and over again in a reaction called a **polymerization**. The longer the chain, the stronger the polymer. These polymers are simple, very long chains. The chain isn't necessarily straight, though; it can twist and turn, like a very long string of cooked spaghetti.

Other polymers, called branched polymers, are a long chain with monomers that stick out to the sides.

Still other polymers are chains that have links between them that tie the polymer chains together. This makes the polymer even stronger because it keeps the chains from sliding over each other These special polymers, called **cross-links**, are like chemical bridges between chains.

DID YOU KNOW?

What do these things have in common?
Frisbees
Fingernails
Latex paint
Nylon clothing
Balloons
Silk, wool, and cotton
Basketballs
Cellulose in plants
Tennis-racquet strings
Plastic grocery bags
Toys
You
They are all made of polymers!

DETERMINATION + LUCK = SUCCESS

Rubber comes from trees that grow in the tropics. The rubber tree has a type of sap, called latex, which oozes out of the bark and can be collected without hurting the tree. Rubber has been used by Indians in North America, Central America, and South America for hundreds of years to make balls and waterproof clothes. When Europeans came to the Americas, they used rubber for the same things. They also used rubber to "rub out" pencil marks, which is where the name comes from.

By the early 1800s, several new companies in Boston, Massachusetts, started making rubber products, such as waterproof raincoats and boots. But the rubber had a problem. A sticky, messy problem. In cold weather, raw rubber becomes stiff; wearing rubber raincoats in a New England winter was like wearing a wooden coat. And in the summer, rubber was even worse. It turned soft and sticky, like glue, and it stank! Not surprisingly, people returned the rubber goods they had bought, and the rubber companies started going out of business in the 1830s. One Boston company even dug a huge pit to bury all of the returned, melting, rubber shoes and coats.

Enter Charles Goodyear. Charles had no background in science, wasn't well known, and he had a lot of debt from a failed hardware store. What Charles did have, though, was a powerful desire to invent things. Charles became fascinated with rubber and how to make it more stable and resistant to changes in temperature. In other words, he wanted to make it useful. He poked and prodded and experimented, adding drying agents, such as magnesium and lime. With another man, Nathaniel Hayward, he figured out how to make rubber more durable by adding sulfur, but it still melted in the heat.

Charles was still in debt, and he was sent to debtors' prison several times for not paying his bills. That didn't stop his work, though; he asked his wife to bring him raw rubber and a rolling pin while he was in prison so he could continue his rubber experiments. He had health problems too, probably from all of the chemicals he used. His family had to catch frogs and turtles for food because there was no money, and sometimes they came up empty handed. But Charles Goodyear was a man obsessed.

Then, one day in 1839, Charles was holding a piece of rubber combined with sulfur while talking with friends near a hot stove. The rubber fell onto the stove, but instead of melting, it became hard! Charles was amazed. Maybe a little bit of heat made rubber melt, but a lot of heat made rubber hard, yet still flexible. Here was the key to making rubber useable.

How much heat worked best? For how long? What was the best way to combine the sulfur? In poor health and broke, he kept experimenting until he produced a rubber that kept its properties in heat and cold. The process of toughening rubber using high heat and chemicals is called **vulcanization**, named after the Roman god of fire, Vulcan.

The vulcanization of rubber is often called one of the great accidental discoveries. But really, it was because Charles persisted in his work despite setbacks, and because his mind was prepared to see the importance of the discovery. There are now over 21 million metric tons of natural and synthetic (manufactured) rubber produced each year. Over half of all manufactured rubber is used for tires; the rest is used for hoses, gloves, and other products. The Goodyear Tire & Rubber Company was named after Charles Goodyear, although he died 30 years before it was founded.

So what does all of this have to do with polymers? Natural, unheated rubber is a polymer, so it has long chains of molecules with some cross-links. When rubber is heated and sulfur is added to it, the sulfur forms many more cross-links between the chains, making it very strong. Rubber is elastic—it bounces back—because the chains are coiled into loops that can stretch out as the rubber bends or stretches, then coil back up when they're released.

WORDS TO KNOW

polymer: a long-chained molecule made up of smaller molecules, called monomers, linked together.

monomer: a small molecule that can link with other monomers to form a polymer.

Kevlar: a polymer fiber that is stronger than steel but very light. It is used to make bullet-proof vests and other body armor.

polymerization: a chemical reaction in which two or more molecules combine to form larger polymer units.

cross-links: chemical bridges, or links, between long polymer chains that make the polymer stiffer.

vulcanization: the process of making rubber tougher using high temperature and chemicals that form cross-links.

dilatant liquid: a liquid that flows more slowly when a force is applied.

suspension: a mixture made up of relatively large particles of a solid within a fluid. The particles settle out if the mixture is undisturbed. Mud and paint are examples of a suspension.

Make Your Own
GOOPY GOOP: OOBLECK

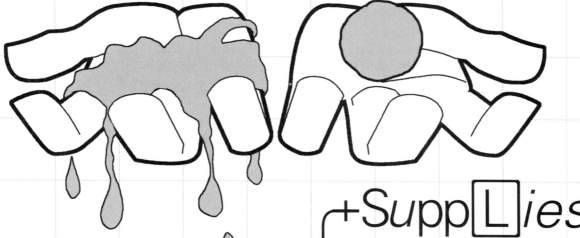

+Supp[L]ies

- **newspaper**
- **1 cup (236 milliliters) cornstarch**
- **bowl**
- **1/2 cup (118 milliliters) water**
- **food coloring (optional)**

Some of the best goop in the world comes straight out of your kitchen. Ask your parents for a good place to try out these recipes, and put down plenty of newspaper. When you're finished, put the goop in a trash can. Never pour it down the drain.

1 Put down newspaper on the table, or do the project outside. Put the cornstarch into the bowl. Slowly add the water, mixing with your fingers until all of the cornstarch is wet. Add a few drops of food coloring if you like. Congratulations! You have just made oobleck!

2 Play with your oobleck. What happens if you squeeze it and then open your hand? Try slapping the oobleck hard, then slowly sinking your fingers into it. Make a ball or roll out a snake and see what happens when you stop rolling. You can adjust your oobleck by adding a little more cornstarch if it feels too wet or more water if it feels too powdery.

What's Happening?

Cornstarch is a polymer. When combined with water, it's also a strange material that doesn't follow the same rules that many other materials do. Most materials will flow faster if more force is applied. For example, if you move your hand through water, when you push harder, the water moves out of the way faster to let your hand through. But cornstarch and water, or oobleck as it's sometimes called, acts differently. When more force is applied, like slapping the oobleck, it becomes harder and resists moving. But when only a small force is applied, like slowly putting your hand in the material, the oobleck acts like a liquid. A liquid that flows more slowly when a force is applied is called **dilatant liquid**. The big question is why this happens. Believe it or not, scientists don't completely understand why, but they have some ideas.

Oobleck is not a simple liquid, like water, but rather is a **suspension**. The particles of cornstarch don't dissolve in water the way salt does; there are still tiny bits of solid cornstarch floating, or suspended, in the water. If you let the mixture sit for a while the cornstarch settles to the bottom.

The size of the cornstarch bits is an important part of why the oobleck suspension is dilatant. The cornstarch particles are all about the same size, a little smaller than the width of a human hair. When hit with a strong force, scientists think that the particles jam together into a cluster, like a log jam, and can't slip past each other. The tiny clusters prevent anything from getting through. But when something moves slowly through oobleck, the particles have time to get out of the way and don't clump.

Researchers are using dilatant liquids to make better bulletproof vests. They're mixing the fluids with materials like Kevlar. The advantage of dilatant fluids is that when a soldier or police officer is moving normally, the fluids move easily, making the armor comfortable to wear. Plain Kevlar is stiff but dilatant fluids are flexible. When a bullet hits with a strong force, though, the liquid acts like a rigid solid and stops the bullet. Materials like this are also being developed to use in skateboard equipment, ski suits, and motorcycle gloves.

JUMPING ON OOBLECK

This involves using a lot more cornstarch and is best done outside, so ask an adult first if it's okay to try. Invite some friends over and amaze them with your ability to walk on water!

1 Figure out how much cornstarch you'll need. If you're using a large plastic tub, you'll probably need about 6 to 10 boxes. A kiddie swimming pool will require 20 to 30 boxes, depending on how deep you want the oobleck. Prepare the mixture following the oobleck directions above, using about half as much water as cornstarch.

2 You can mix it up directly in the plastic tub or pool. If you're working inside, spread out LOTS of newspaper under the container. Try to make the mixture at least 2 inches (5 centimeters) deep. Take off your shoes and socks and jump as hard as you can. Can you run across it? Anyone for hopscotch?

3 When you're done, don't dump the oobleck down the drain. Let it dry out. You can either save if for another time (just add water and you're ready to go) or place it in the trash.

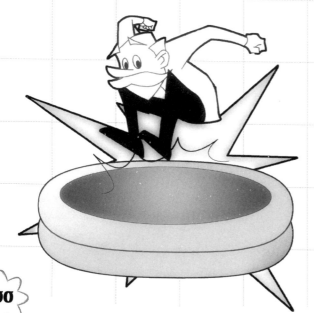

+Supp[L]ies

- lots of newspaper if you're working inside
- cornstarch (anywhere from 6 to 30 boxes, depending on the size of tub)
- large plastic tub or kiddie plastic swimming pool
- water
- measuring cup
- food coloring (optional)

SILLY GOOP

1 In a paper cup, mix the glue, 4 tablespoons (60 milliliters) water, and a few drops of food coloring. Add 1 tablespoon (15 milliliters) borax and the cornstarch and mix well.

2 In another cup, mix two-thirds cup (158 milliliters) water and 2 teaspoons (10 milliliters) borax until the borax dissolves. Pour 2 tablespoons (30 milliliters) of the borax and water solution into the glue mixture and stir until it's stiff.

3 Let the mixture set for a minute, then take it out of the cup and rinse with water. Blot the extra water with a paper towel and knead the mixture until it's smooth. If you want it to be stiffer, add more of the borax and water solution. What does your silly goop do? Try bouncing it, breaking it, stretching it. Does it keep its shape? Is it hard or soft or both?

+SuppLies

- 2 paper cups
- measuring spoons
- 4 tablespoons (60 milliliters) white wood glue, such as Elmer's
- warm water
- food coloring (optional)
- 1 tablespoon and 2 teaspoons (25 milliliters total) borax powder, from the laundry section of the grocery store
- 1 tablespoon (15 milliliters) cornstarch
- spoon

What's Happening

Silly goop is a polymer. The glue contains a polymer, polyvinyl acetate (PVA), which is made from monomers of vinyl acetate. So the glue is a polymer to start with, but when the borax is added, the chains cross-link to make even bigger—and stiffer—polymer chains. Cross-links are like chemical bridges between chains, linking them together. Cross-links make a polymer stiffer because the chains can't slide past each other and separate since they're hooked together. Knowing how and why the borax works will help you to vary the ingredients to get goop with different qualities.

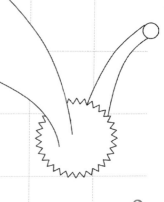

Make Your Own
MERINGUE COOKIES

Caution: This activity involves using an electric mixer and an oven, so get an adult to help.

Meringue is that white, fluffy-looking stuff you see on the tops of some cakes and pies, like lemon meringue pie—yum! Meringue is not only delicious, it's a fascinating polymer. This recipe for meringue cookies works best if you make the cookies on a cool, dry day. In hot, humid weather, the meringue doesn't dry properly.

1 Preheat the oven to 250 degrees Fahrenheit (121 degrees Celsius) and put the oven rack in the middle of the oven. Line a cookie sheet with wax paper. Hold an egg lightly with one hand, and with the other hand, crack the eggshell firmly with the butter knife.

2 Pull the egg apart without letting the yolk fall into the bowl. Pour the yolk back and forth between the eggshell halves. Let the egg white fall into one small bowl, but keep the yolk in the shell and be careful that the yolk doesn't break. When all of the white is in the bowl, put the yolk into the other small bowl. You can save the yolks for another cooking project or throw them away. Now pour the white from the small bowl into the large bowl, so that if you break a yolk on another egg, you won't ruin the whole batch.

+Supp[L]ies

- oven
- cookie sheet
- wax paper
- 6 eggs at room temperature
- butter knife
- 2 small bowls
- large metal or glass bowl
- 1/4 teaspoon (1 milliliter) cream of tartar or white vinegar
- electric mixer
- 1/2 cup (118 milliliters) sugar
- 1/4 teaspoon (1 milliliter) vanilla (optional)

3 Repeat step 2 for the rest of the eggs. When the egg whites are all in the large bowl, add the cream of tartar or vinegar. Beat the mixture with an electric mixer on high until the egg whites get foamy and form soft peaks that gently flop over when you remove the beaters.

4 Gradually add the sugar and vanilla extract and keep beating just until the meringue is shiny, smooth, and stands up in a peak about 2 inches (5 centimeters) high.

5 Drop big blobs of the meringue onto the wax paper on the cookie sheet and bake for 1 hour 30 minutes. The meringues should look dry, stiff, and very light brown. Turn off the oven and let the meringue cookies cool completely in the oven before you take them out—at least one hour.

6 Clean up carefully! You don't get to lick the bowl in this recipe because raw eggs can make you sick. For the same reason, make sure you use paper towels to wipe up any spilled raw egg, then throw them in the trash.

7 Try the recipe different ways. What happens if you use eggs that are right out of the refrigerator and still cold? What if you add lots and lots of sugar? What if you leave out the cream of tartar (or vinegar)? What if you use a plastic bowl? Remember: make one change at a time so you know which change made which difference.

What's Happening?

Egg whites are mostly water—about 88 percent. The rest is almost all protein, which is a polymer. The protein molecules are tightly wound, a bit like dry angel hair pasta or a Slinky®. When you whip the egg whites, the proteins unfold and stretch, forming a network of bubbles. This unwinding of the protein is called denaturing. The proteins begin to overlap as you whip the eggs even more, forming a long, stretchy surface. Eventually, the structure becomes more rigid. This is what makes the egg whites form stiff peaks. Cream of tartar and vinegar are acids that help the egg whites unwind. The heat from the oven "sets" the egg whites, which means that it makes the proteins unite and makes the structure rigid.

Water is all around us. It's in the paper used for this book. It's in the furniture we sit on. It's in the air. And it's in you. Almost everything you can see and touch has at least a tiny amount of water in it.

You might think that because water is everywhere, it's a very simple substance. Not true! Water has some very unusual properties. That's a good thing because those unusual properties make it possible for us to skate on frozen ponds, for fish to survive the winter, for plants to grow, and even for there to be life at all.

Water, Water
Everywhere

We've talked a lot about water in earlier chapters, so you may recall that water is sometimes called H_2O because it's made up of two hydrogen atoms and one oxygen atom. Look at the diagram to the right; the oxygen atom has a minus sign on it and the hydrogen atoms have a plus sign. That's because the oxygen atom has a stronger pull on the electrons, which have a negative charge, and pulls them closer. So the area around the oxygen atom is negative, and the

DID YOU KNOW?

Sir James Dewar, a Scottish chemist and physicist, made a disc of soap film that lasted over three years!

WHERE'S WATER?

⦿ Your body is mostly water, although the amount decreases as you get older. When you were a baby, about 74 percent of your body was water. At age 10, about 60 percent of your body is water. When you're 70 years old, about 56 percent will be water if you're male and about 47 percent if you're female.

⦿ Water covers about 71 percent of the surface of the earth. Most of it is in the oceans and ice at the North and South Poles, but water is also in clouds, rain, rivers, lakes, and in underground **aquifers**.

⦿ In outer space, frozen water, or ice, has been found on the moon, on planets— particularly Mercury, Mars, Neptune, and Pluto—and in comets and clouds between stars in our galaxy. Recent explorations of Mars indicate that there may be liquid water underground on Mars. This means there could be **microorganisms** living there!

areas around the hydrogen atoms are positive. When one end of a molecule has a slight negative charge and one end a positive charge, the molecule is polar. The **polarity** also gives water molecules a shape like a "V."

Since positive and negative charges are attracted to each other, the oxygen end of a water molecule is attracted to the hydrogen end of other water molecules. The oxygen end is also attracted to other positively charged particles—like the sodium in salt. Because of this, water's polarity allows it to dissolve many substances that humans and animals need and to transport them to different parts of the body.

Surface Tension

Try putting a drop of water on wax paper or glass and look at it closely. Does it look like it has a skin? There really isn't a skin; what you're seeing is **surface tension**. The molecules in water are attracted to each other, like tiny magnets, because the hydrogen atom in one molecule is attracted to the oxygen atom in another molecule. Every water molecule feels pulled towards the others, so the water molecules shrink away from the surface and cling to each other.

Surface tension causes water to take the shape that has the smallest surface area, which is why a drop of water takes the shape of a sphere. Try the projects at the end of the chapter to see just how strong surface tension can be or what happens when the surface tension of water is lowered.

Expanding Water

When water freezes, it expands, or gets bigger. This may not seem like a big deal but it is. Nearly every other liquid shrinks when it becomes a solid. That's because a liquid has more energy than a solid, and the molecules usually need more room to move around. When water freezes, the oxygen atom bonds with two more hydrogen atoms so that it is bonded to four altogether, like the picture to the right. This structure actually takes up slightly more space than the liquid and it means that ice is less dense than water.

So what? Because ice is less dense, it floats on top of water. When pond water freezes, the ice floats on top and the water beneath is insulated from the colder air. People can skate on the ice on top, and fish can live underneath in cold, but not frozen, water. If ice were heavier than water, it would sink to the bottom, and the water above would not be insulated. The entire pond would freeze.

DID YOU KNOW?

Eiffel Plasterer, a high school science teacher who experimented with bubbles, blew a bubble that lasted for 341 days!

AGNES POCKELS: KITCHEN CHEMIST

Agnes Pockels was born in Germany in 1862. At that time, women in that country could not go to college. Agnes loved science and excelled in school, so when women were later allowed to attend college, she wanted to go. But her parents became ill with malaria and she needed to be home to take care of them. Agnes stayed interested in science, however, reading any textbooks she could find and trying out her own experiments. While washing dishes, she studied the surface tension of water and noticed that different things affected the surface tension. Using bowls, string, and buttons, she made the first-ever device to measure surface tension.

Because Agnes didn't have a college degree and was unknown in the world of science, she couldn't publish a paper about her findings, so she sent her information to Lord Rayleigh, the same scientist who followed up on Benjamin Franklin's experiments with oil and water (see page 61). Lord Rayleigh was so impressed with her work that he sent it to *Nature* magazine, a famous science journal, which published the letter. She continued her research on surfaces and solutions for over 40 years, publishing more papers on her own and winning awards. Some of her methods are still used today. Agnes did all of her work in the laboratory at her home—her kitchen!

TRY THIS: ICE SPIKES!

Fill an ice cube tray with distilled water from the grocery store or rain water. When you place it in the freezer, it will often form spikes, sometimes as long as an inch. Why? The surface of the water first becomes covered in ice, growing from the outside edge in, until only a small hole is left in the middle. Ice takes up more space than water, so as more ice forms underneath, the water that's left has nowhere to go and it's forced up through the hole. Bit by bit, more water is pushed up through the hole, and it freezes into a spike. Try using containers of different sizes and shapes. If you live in an area where it snows in winter, try this experiment outside at different temperatures to see what happens.

DIAGRAM OF AN ICE MOLECULE—
LOOKING DOWN ON IT.

DID YOU KNOW?

Surface tension is part of the reason that insects commonly known as water striders can rest on a pond, or skim across it, without sinking. Their legs have thousands of tiny hairs, each about two-thousandths of an inch (five hundredths of a milliliter) long. The hairs have tiny grooves that trap air. All those tiny hairs are held up by the surface tension of the water.

WORDS TO KNOW

aquifer: rocks, sands, or gravels, located underground, that contain water.

microorganism: anything living that is so small you can only see it with a microscope.

polarity: the quality of a molecule having one end with a negative charge, and the other end with a positive charge.

surface tension: the force that holds together molecules on the surface of a liquid so that the liquid acts like it has a stretchy skin. Water has a high surface tension.

surfactant: short for "surface active agent." A substance that lowers the surface tension of a liquid, such as soap.

107

DID YOU KNOW?

Frei Otto, an architect and engineer, used soap bubbles and films as models for the tent-like buildings he designed, because soap films always use the least area.

What's in a Bubble?

If you turn on the water full blast in the kitchen sink and look closely, you'll see bubbles form and disappear very quickly. That's because the surface tension pulls on the bubble and makes it collapse. If you add dish soap, it lowers the surface tension, and the bubbles last much longer. But what really IS a bubble? It's two layers of soap molecules—**surfactant**—surrounding a layer of water molecules. The film of a soap bubble is about the thinnest thing that you can see with just your own eyes. It's about 5,000 times thinner than a human hair. Soap films always take up the smallest area possible, which means a bubble is always a sphere.

BABY LUNGS

Our lungs use small air sacs, like balloons, to breathe. These air sacs are coated with water and a natural surfactant. Water has a high surface tension, so these tiny air sacs would collapse when we breathe out if they didn't have surfactant—just like water bubbles collapse without dish soap. And every new breath would take a lot of force, like blowing up a new balloon.

Premature babies do not have enough of this surfactant, and their lungs can't expand on their own. Understanding surface tension has allowed doctors to manufacture surfactants to help these babies breathe until they can make their own.

Make Your Own
MARBLEIZED PAPER

1 Spread out the newspaper and place the pan on top of it. Spread extra newspaper as a drying area. Pour a thin layer of milk in the pan, enough to cover the entire bottom of the pan.

2 Add a few drops of food coloring in the center of the pan. Add a few drops of a second color next to the first color. Add a drop or two of the dish soap in between the two colors. The colors will zoom to the outside of the pan.

3 Very gently and slowly drag the stick or fork through the colors. See if you can get thin tendrils of color to swirl around. Look closely at the drop of soap; do you see color flowing away from it?

4 Place a sheet of paper flat onto the surface design and quickly take it off again. Lay the paper, color side up, on the newspaper to dry. Swirl the colors around some more until they become gray, then dump the milk and food color mixture into the sink. Try it again with different colors. What happens if you try it with water or cream instead of milk?

What's Happening?

The food coloring is mostly water, with some pigment mixed in. Water is less dense than milk, so the food coloring floats. The dishwashing soap reduces the surface tension of the water and the milk. The soap molecules push their way between the water molecules at the surface, making the food coloring zoom away from the soap.

Make Your Own
WATER THAT BENDS

1 Hold the paper clip or needle vertically and drop it into the water. It should sink because metal paper clips are denser than water.

2 Take the paper clip out. Hold it flat and slowly lower it onto the water. The paper clip should stay on top of the water now. If it sinks, try lowering it gently with a fork.

3 Look closely at the water around the paper clip. Do you see the water bend as it touches the paper clip? You probably never thought that water could bend! Add a drop of dish soap to the surface of the water near the paper clip. Now what happens?

+Supp[L]ies

- **small bowl of water**
- **metal paper clip or needle**
- **fork**
- **liquid dish washing soap**

What's Happening?

The paper clip is not actually floating. If it could float, it would do so no matter how you put it in the water. But when you slowly lower the paper clip, it lightly rests on the "skin" of the water, held up by the force of the surface tension. The surface tension has enough force to counteract the force of gravity that pulls on the paper clip. Which force—surface tension or gravity—would win out if you put a marble on top of the water? Try different objects. Do they sink or float or are they held up by surface tension? Why does the soap make the paper clip sink? Because the soap molecules reduce the surface tension of the water by squeezing their way in between the water molecules.

Make Your Own
BUBBLE SOLUTION

Bubble Fun 1

Try making your own bubble solution, then try some of the following different ways of making bubbles. If you're working indoors, put down newspaper first. Bubble stuff is slippery!

1 Pour the water into the container. Gently but thoroughly mix the dishwashing soap into the water.

2 Skim off any foam from the top. Add the corn syrup or glycerin. After letting the bubble solution sit for a day, make some bubbles. Hold your hands in a hoop shape. Dip your hands in the bubble solution and pull them out. Gently blow, and when you have a bubble you like, close your hands.

Tips for Longer-Lasting Bubbles

- Add glycerin or corn syrup (corn syrup costs less).
- Use distilled water or rain water, especially if you have "hard" water.
- Let the bubble solution sit for one or more days.
- Keep dust out of the solution. Cover it when you're not using it.
- Make bubbles when it's humid and there's no wind.
- Try blowing a bubble and putting it in a closed container to see how long it will last. Make sure to rub bubble solution onto every surface in the container first.
- Try different concoctions to see what works best!

+Supp[L]ies

- shallow container, like a pie pan or baking dish
- 1/2 gallon (2 liters) of water
- 3/4 (177 milliliters) cup liquid dishwashing soap, like Dawn or Joy
- 1/4 cup (59 milliliters) glycerin or corn syrup

111

Bubble Fun 2

1 Place the bubble solution on the plastic sheets or newspaper. Cut the string about six times as long as one straw. Pull the string through each of the straws so that you have a rectangle, with the straws on opposite sides and plenty of string between the straws. Knot the string to form a loop.

2 Hold one straw in each hand, and dip the rectangle into the bubble solution. Lift up and slowly pull the straws apart. You should have a soap film.

3 Hold the frame in front of you, just below your waist. Pull the frame up and slightly towards you. If you need to, walk slowly backwards as you pull. To release the bubble, pull the frame up as you bring the straws together. You can also try twisting the straws in opposite directions. Practice over and over!

+SuppLies

- **plastic sheets or newspaper to put under the pan if you're doing this indoors**
- **scissors**
- **cotton string**
- **2 drinking straws**
- **bubble solution in a large, shallow pan**

IT'S COLD OUT THERE!

If you live where it gets cold in the winter, try this: When it's very, very cold (about 10 degrees Fahrenheit/-12 degrees Celsius or colder), make up some bubble solution and blow bubbles. The thin layer of water between the soap layers freezes before the bubble bursts. Try making bubbles by sweeping your wand through the air, and also by blowing bubbles. Which freezes first? Your breath is warm, so it takes longer to freeze. It also makes the bubble crumple because when the warm air hits the cold, it contracts, or gets smaller, as it cools. This makes the skin of the bubble crumple.

The inside is filled with gas—plain air for the ones you wave through the air, mostly carbon dioxide for the ones you blow.

Bubble Fun 3

1 Pour the bubble solution into the cookie sheet and dip the straw into the solution. Hold the straw just above the bubble solution and blow gently. When you have a bubble almost as big as a tennis ball, pull the straw out. Poke the bubble with a dry pencil. What happens? Blow another bubble, get the pencil wet, and poke it.

2 Carefully push the wet end of the straw into the bubble until it touches the bubble mix on the cookie sheet. Slowly blow a bubble inside the first bubble. Can you blow more than one bubble inside the first one?

3 Try blowing very gently or very quickly into the bubble solution, exploring different kinds of bubbles. Use different shapes to blow bubbles. You can form the pipe cleaners into stars, letters, boxes, or any other shape as long as the shape is closed.

4 You have already used a straw, which is a narrow tube shape. Try using a bigger tube shape to make a bigger bubble. You can use a toilet paper roll (until it gets soggy!) or a tin can open at both ends as a tube. Just make sure there aren't any sharp edges on the tin can. Dip one end of your tube into the bubble solution to get a film, then blow gently from the other end. When you get a bubble, gently twist the tube to release the bubble. You can also try making an even longer tube from two or more cans taped together.

+Supp[L]ies
- **bubble solution**
- **short-sided cookie sheet**
- **drinking straw**
- **pencil**
- **pipe cleaners, tin cans, cardboard toilet-paper roll, hollow tube-shaped objects (optional)**

Bubble Fun 4

1 It's best to do this outdoors in the grass, but if there's any wind or it's too cold, you can do it indoors if you have permission. Spread out a thick plastic sheet, and place the newspapers on top (the bubble solution is too slippery on plastic). Place the baby pool on top of the newspapers.

2 If you have some cloth or yarn, wind it around the Hula Hoop, overlapping the edges of the cloth. You can use the Hula Hoop without this, but the materials help hold more bubble solution, making bigger bubbles. Set the crate in the baby pool, and place the Hula Hoop around the crate.

3 Ask one person to step onto the crate, with hands by his or her side. You and another person stand on either side, outside the pool, and wet your hands. Make sure the Hula Hoop and cloth are completely wet, and then pull it up over the first person's head. Try pulling at different speeds to see what works best. How tall can you make the bubble?

+SuppLies

- 2 friends or family members
- round kiddie swimming pool, slightly larger around than a Hula Hoop
- thick plastic sheet and newspapers if you're doing this inside
- Hula Hoop
- cloth in strips or yarn (optional)
- step stool or crate
- bubble solution with corn syrup or glycerin, enough to fill the pool about 3 inches (8 centimeters) deep

What's Happening?

A soap solution contains soap molecules and water molecules. The soap molecules have a "head" that has a negative charge and a "tail" that does not have a charge. The head loves water (because water has a charge too) and wants to be in it, but the tail hates water and wants to be out of it. So these soap molecules crowd to the surface, where part of the molecule can be in water and part out of it. The soap molecules squeeze their way between the water molecules. Because the water molecules are farther apart, they don't pull on each other as strongly, so the force of the surface tension is reduced.

Glossary

acid: a substance that donates a hydrogen ion (H⁺) to another substance. Examples include vinegar, and lemon juice.

activation energy: the energy that starts a chemical reaction.

amorphous solid: a solid where the atoms are in a mostly random, but still tightly bonded, arrangement.

aquifer: rocks, sands, or gravels, located underground, that contain water.

Archimedes's Principle: when an object is placed in a fluid, it experiences an upward force that is equal to the weight of the fluid that is displaced.

atmosphere: the blanket of air surrounding Earth.

atom: the smallest particle of matter that cannot be broken down by chemical means. An atom is made up of a nucleus of protons and neutrons, surrounded by a cloud of electrons.

atomic number: the number of protons in the nucleus of an atom. The atomic number is used to distinguish elements in the periodic table of elements.

base: a substance that accepts a hydrogen ion (H⁺) from another substance. Examples include baking soda, ammonia, and oven cleaner.

boiling point: the temperature at which a liquid boils, or turns to a gas. Different substances have different boiling points. This is the same as the condensation point.

bond: an attractive force that holds together the atoms, ions, or groups of atoms in a molecule.

carbon: an element found in all living things.

chemical formula: a representation of a substance or of a chemical reaction using symbols for its elements.

chemical reaction: the rearrangement of atoms in a substance to make a new chemical substance.

chemistry: the study of the properties of substances and how they react with one another.

chromatography: a method of separating the components of a mixture by differences in their attraction to a liquid or gas.

compound: a substance made up of two or more elements. The elements are held together by bonds just as molecules are held together by bonds. Compounds are not easily separated. Water is a compound.

corrosion: the wearing away of metal by a chemical reaction. Rust is a type of corrosion.

cross-links: chemical bridges, or links, between long polymer chains that make the polymer stiffer.

crystal: a solid where the atoms are arranged in a highly ordered pattern.

density: the amount of matter in a given space, or mass divided by volume.

diatomaceous earth: a light material that comes from diatom (fossilized) remains of algae. It is nonreactive.

dilatant liquid: a liquid that flows more slowly when a force is applied.

displace: to remove or take the place of.

electrical charge: a fundamental property of matter. Protons and the nuclei of atoms have a positive charge, electrons have a negative charge, and neutrons have no charge. Normally, each atom has as many protons as electrons and thus has no net electrical charge—the atom is neutral.

electron: a stable, negatively charged particle found in all atoms.

element: a substance whose atoms are all the same. Examples of elements include gold, oxygen, and carbon.

elevation: height above sea level.

endothermic reaction: a chemical reaction that absorbs energy. An example is photosynthesis in plants, which absorbs energy from the sun.

exothermic reaction: a chemical reaction that releases energy, usually in the form of heat. An example is a burning log.

formic acid: a liquid acid found in and produced by ants and many plants.

gas: one of the three states of matter where the particles are not bound to each other and move very fast in all directions. A gas does not have a definite shape or volume.

gas pressure: the force of gas molecules hitting the surface of a container.

geometric arrangements: crystal systems, or ways in which crystals are arranged. There are seven geometric arrangements.

heat: the total energy from the motion of all of the particles in a substance.

hemoglobin: a substance in red blood cells that combines with and carries oxygen around the body, and gives blood its red color.

hexagon: a plane figure with six straight sides and angles.

hydroxyl group: an (OH⁻) ion, often found in bases.

ion: an atom that has an unequal number of protons and electrons. Ions have either a positive or negative charge.

Kevlar: a polymer fiber that is stronger than steel, but very light. It is used to make bullet-proof vests and other body armor.

latent heat: the heat that is released or absorbed when a substance changes its state.

liquid: one of the three states of matter where the particles cluster together and flow. A liquid has a definite volume, but takes the shape of its container.

mass: the amount of matter or "stuff" in something. On Earth, the mass of something is very close to its weight.

matter: the material substance of the universe that has mass, occupies space, and can change (convert) into energy.

melting point: the temperature at which a solid melts, or turns to a liquid. Different substances have different melting points. Also the freezing point.

microorganism: anything living that is so small you can only see it with a microscope.

mixture: a substance that has two or more different kinds of materials mixed together but not bonded together. Air, muddy water, or brass—a mixture of zinc and copper—are mixtures.

molecule: the simplest structural unit of an element or compound, a group of atoms bonded together. Molecules can break apart and form new ones, which is a chemical reaction.

monomer: a small molecule that can link with other monomers to form polymers.

neon: a gas used in fluorescent lighting that gives an orange glow when electricity is passed through it.

neurotoxic: poisonous to nerves or nerve tissues, like the brain.

neutralization: a reaction between an acid and a base that uses up all of the acid and base. The products of the reaction are water and a salt and have a neutral pH of seven.

neutron: a particle of an atom that is found in the nucleus of all atoms and has no electrical charge.

nuclear reaction: a process in which two nuclei or nuclear particles collide to produce products different from the initial particles.

nucleus: the central part of an atom, made up of protons and neutrons.

particle: a very small portion of matter such as a molecule, atom, or electron.

Pascal's Principle: when a liquid or gas is pushed on by a force, it transmits the force to all parts of the fluid.

pentagon: a plane figure with five straight sides and angles.

periodic table of elements: a table that arranges all of the elements according to their properties.

pH: a measure of how acidic or basic a substance is. The pH measures how many hydrogen ions are in a substance, and ranges from 0 to 14.

phase change: the change of one state of matter (solid, liquid, or gas) to another.

pitch: a substance that is made from tar.

plasma: a state of matter under high heat or pressure where the electrons have been stripped away.

polarity: the quality of a molecule having one end with a negative charge and the other end with a positive charge.

polymer: a long-chained molecule made up of smaller molecules, called monomers, linked together.

polymerization: a chemical reaction in which two or more molecules combine to form larger polymer units.

products: the new substances formed from a chemical reaction.

properties: unique characteristics of a substance.

proton: a type of elementary particle that has a positive electrical charge and is found in the nucleus of all atoms.

pure substance: a substance in which all of the molecules are the same, such as pure gold or a quartz crystal.

quintillion: The cardinal number with 18 zeros after it.

reactants: the substances that are being changed in a chemical reaction.

solid: one of the three states of matter where the particles are bound tightly. A solid has a definite shape and volume and does not flow.

solute: the dissolved substance in a solution.

solution: a mixture of two or more substances; often but not always a liquid solution.

state of matter: the form that matter takes. There are three common states of matter: solid, liquid, and gas.

sublimation: the change of a solid directly to a gas, without passing through the liquid phase.

substance: physical material from which something is made.

supercooling: when a liquid cools below its melting/freezing point without turning to a solid.

supercritical fluid: gas that is at such a high temperature (the critical temperature) that it cannot turn into liquid.

surface tension: the force that holds the molecules together on the surface of a liquid, so that the liquid acts like it has a stretchy skin. Water has a high surface tension.

surfactant: short for "surface active agent." A substance that lowers the surface tension of a liquid, such as soap.

suspension: a mixture made up of relatively large particles of a solid within a liquid. The particles settle out if the mixture is undisturbed.

temperature: a measure of the average energy, or speed, of all of the particles in a substance.

tetrahedron: a shape with four triangular faces.

vacuum: a space that is empty of matter.

variable: something that can vary or change.

viscosity: the resistance to flow of a fluid. A liquid that is very viscous, such as honey, flows slowly.

void: a large hole or empty space.

volume: the amount of space occupied by something.

vulcanization: the process of making rubber tougher using high temperature and chemicals that form cross-links.

water vapor: the gas state of water.

Books

Aldersey-Williams, Hugh. *The Most Beautiful Molecule: The Discovery of the Buckyball*. New York: John Wiley & Sons, 1995.

Ardley, Neil. *101 Great Science Experiments*. New York: Dorling Kindersly, 2006.

Bendick, Jeanne. *Archimedes and the Door of Science*. Warsaw: Bethlehem Books, 1997.

Boorstin, Daniel J. *The Discoverers: A History of Man's Search to Know His World and Himself.* New York: Vintage Books, 1985.

Boys, C.V. *Soap Bubbles and the Forces Which Mould Them*. New York: Doubleday & Company, Inc., 1959.

Buddemeier, R., Dleypas, J.A., and Aronson, R. "Coral Reefs & Climate Change: Potential Contributions of Climate Change to Stresses on Coral Reef Ecosystems." (2004) Prepared for the Pew Center on Global Climate Change, 56 pp.

Downie, Neil A. *Exploding disk cannons, slimemobiles, and 43 other projects for Saturday science*. Baltimore: Johns Hopkins University Press, 2006.

"Found It! Ice on Mars." (28 February 2002) [Accessed February 22, 2007] http://science.nasa.gov/headlines/y2002/28may_marsice.htm.

Franklin, Benjamin, "Of the stilling of Waves by means of oil." (1774) *Philosophical Transactions of the Royal Society* 64: 445-60.

Frederickson, M., M.J. Greene and D.M. Gordon. "Ants bedevil devil's gardens." (2005) *Nature* 437:495–496.

Green, Martin Burgess, *Gandhi*. New York: Continuum, 1993.

Hakim, Joy. *The Story of Science: Aristotle Leads the Way*. Washington, Smithsonian Books, 2004.

Hakim, Joy. *The Story of Science: Einstein Adds a New Dimension*. Washington: Smithsonian Books, 2007.

Hakim, Joy. *The Story of Science: Newton at the Center*. Washington: Smithsonian Books, 2005.

Hoffman, Roald. *The Same and Not the Same*. New York: Columbia Press, 1995.

Jeng, M., 2005. "Hot Water Can Freeze Faster Than Cold?!?" PhysicsarXiv:physics/0512262, v.1 (29 Dec 2005) [accessed March 20, 2007] http://arxiv.org/PS_cache/physics/pdf/0512/0512262v1.pdf.

Kleypas, J.A., R.A. Feely, V.J. Fabry, C. Langdon, C.L. Sabine, and L.L. Robbins, 2006. Impacts of Ocean Acidification on Coral Reefs and Other Marine Calcifiers: A Guide for Future Research, report of a workshop held 18–20 April 2005, St. Petersburg, FL, sponsored by NSF, NOAA, and the U.S. Geological Survey, 88 pp.

Langone, John. *Theories for everything: an illustrated history of science from the invention of numbers to string theory*. Washington, D.C.: National Geographic, 2006.

Mainstone, J., "An Improbable Journey from Cambridge to Cambridge." (2005) *Australian Physics* Vol. 42, No. 2.

"Making a Splash on Mars." 29 (June 2000) [Accessed February 24, 2007] http://science.nasa.gov/headlines/y2000/ast29jun_1m.htm.

Malik, T., "Changing Mars Gullies Hint at Recent Flowing Water." (12 June 2006) [Accessed February 27, 2007] http://www.space.com/scienceastronomy/061206_mars_gullies.html.

Mestel, Rosie. "Hitch's birds deranged by dodgy anchovies (toxicity of domoic acid in Alfred Hitchcock's seabirds)." *New Scientist* 147.n1987 (July 22, 1995): 6(1). *Expanded Academic ASAP.* Thomson Gale. EIN Remote Access. 29 Mar. 2007.

Mpemba, E.B. and Osborne, D.G., "Cool?." (1969) *Phys. Educ.* 4, 172–175.

Noddy, Tom. *Tom Noddy's Bubble Magic.* Philadelphia, Pennsylvania: Running Press, 1988.

Plimpton, George. *Fireworks: A History and Celebration.* New York: Doubleday & Company, Inc., 1984.

Roach, John, "Ants Use Acid to Make Gardens in Amazon, Study Says" *National Geographic News,* 2006. (09 September 2005) [accessed on March 21, 2007] http://news.nationalgeographic.com/news/2005/09/0921_050921_amazon_ant.html

Safer by the Sip: "Nano-rust" Cleans Arsenic from Drinking Water. [Accessed on March 12, 2007,] http://cohesion.rice.edu/CentersAndInst/CBEN/emplibrary/Rice%20NSEC%20EEC-0647452%20Arsenic%20removal%20using%20nanorust%20(summary).pdf

Silver, Brian. *The Ascent of Science.* New York: Oxford University Press, 1998.

Smith, Alastair, ed., *Usborne Big Book of Experiments.* New York: Usborne Publishing, 1996.

Susan McKeever, ed., *The DK Science Encyclopedia.* New York: DK Publishing, 1998.

Tanford, Charles. *Ben Franklin Stilled the Waves: An Informal History of Pouring Oil on Water with Reflections on the Ups and Downs of Scientific Life in General.* New York: Oxford University Press, 2004.

Walker, J. "The Amateur Scientist: Hot Water Freezes Faster Than Cold Water. Why Does It Do So?" (1977) *Scientific American* 237 (3): 246–257.

Wolf, Charles. *Chemistry Applied and Descriptive.* Dallas: J.M. LeBel Enterprises, 2002.

Zubrowski, Bernie. *Bubbles: A Children's Museum Activity Book.* Boston: Little, Brown & Co., 1979.

Web Sites

History of Science and Chemistry:

Information and interview with Stephanie Kwolek, the inventor of Kevlar, as well as other scientists. http://web.mit.edu/invent/www/ima/kwolek_video.html

Information on Charles Goodyear, the discovery of rubber, and the history of the Goodyear Tire Company. http://www.goodyear.com/corporate/history/history_story.html

History of Science (information on lots of scientists, organized by subject). http://www.woodrow.org/teachers/ci/1992/

Contributions of 20th Century Women to Physics, including Agnes Pockels. http://cwp.library.ucla.edu/

Chemical Achievers (biographies of many chemists from the Chemical Heritage Foundation).
http://www.chemheritage.org/classroom/chemach/index.html

Information on secret codes, invisible ink, and captured letters from the American Revolution.
http://www.si.umich.edu/spies/index-methods.html

Story of the Gold Medal and Nazis, as well as other Nobel laureate stories.
http://nobelprize.org/nobel_prizes/medals/

Activities and Demonstrations:

Tons of fun science activities with explanations, www.exploratorium.edu

Chemistry Comes Alive! Video collection of explosions and other chemistry experiments from the Journal of Chemical Education.
http://jchemed.chem.wisc.edu/JCESoft/CCA/pirelli/index.html

Bubbles, bubbles, and more bubbles, from an expert in the art of making them.
http://www.tomnoddy.com/

If you have some time, a handy adult to help, and the desire to make a giant soap film.
http://maartenrutgers.org/fun/howto/howto.html

Everything you ever wanted to know about polymers, especially for kids.
http://www.pslc.ws/macrog.htm

Theory and Information:

Periodic Table (click on each element to find out more information): http://www.chemicool.com/
3-D Interactive Structure of many Molecules. http://www.3dchem.com/index.asp

Northwest Fisheries Science Center, Harmful Algal Blooms Program.
http://www.nwfsc.noaa.gov/hab/index.html

DK Online Encyclopedia that links to kid-friendly science websites with downloadable images for reports. This website can be used alone, or with DK's linked book, *E.encyclopedia.science*.
http://www.science.dke-encyc.com/home.asp

For additional information about sources used in the research for this book, please send requests to:

Cynthia Light Brown

c/o Nomad Press

2456 Christian Street

White River Junction, VT 05001

Index